In God's Embrace
A Story of Faith, Love, and Loss

Steven M. Darr

Copyright © 2024

All Rights Reserved

Dedication

To my Lord and Savior, Jesus Christ,

In humble gratitude, I dedicate this book to You. Your grace has been the ink that fills the pages of my life, and Your love has been the guiding light illuminating the words within these chapters. May this work be a testament to Your enduring presence and the transformative power of Your Word.

I also dedicate this book to my family and friends, who have supported me with unwavering faith and love. Your prayers and encouragement have been a source of strength, and I am grateful for the community of believers who have walked alongside me on this literary journey.

May the words written here reflect Your truth, inspire hearts, and draw readers closer to Your infinite love. May it be a small offering, a fragrant offering, in response to the boundless grace You have poured into my life.

Amen.

Acknowledgements

I would like to express my deepest love and gratitude to my wife, Faith, whose unwavering support and gentle guidance were instrumental in bringing this book to fruition.

I am also indebted to Judy for her assistance and feedback throughout the editing and proofreading of the book and for her belief in the importance of this project.

Special thanks to Jonathan for his expertise in design and for generously sharing his insights, which greatly enriched the production of this book.

Lastly, to all those who have inspired and influenced me along my faith journey whether through conversations, books, or experiences, your impact is woven into the fabric of these pages.

This book would not have been possible without the collective support and contributions of each individual mentioned above. Thank you for being an integral part of this creative endeavor.

About the Author

Steven has served as the Lead Pastor at First Congregational Church of Torrington, CT, for nearly 20 years. He attended the Southern Baptist Theological Seminary, where he received his Master of Divinity Degree in 2005. Steven is a descendant of Ann Harnden, the young woman of whom this book is written. Upon discovery of the original letters from the 1840s that are referenced in the book, Steven embarked upon the writing of Ann's story. This story of faith, love, and loss has been written to inspire others to trust in God through all aspects of their lives. In 2012, Steven accompanied Rev. Peter Smith, a friend and mentor, on a mission trip to India. There, he learned firsthand the trials and the joys of being a missionary to a foreign land. Steven would go back to India if the opportunity arrived. There is such a hunger for the Word of God. He and his wife Faith live in Torrington, CT, where their love of greyhounds has provided them with years of enjoyment in caring for these retired racers.

Preface

My father, Chester Darr, loved his family. He had grown up in a broken family, so the family he created was near and dear to him. He lived that out each day of his life. Along with my mother, he raised five boys who also loved family. Dad was deeply into genealogy. He traveled around the United States checking out gravestones and doing rubbings on those he considered important to the family. He and his nephew, George Mason, created a wonderful chart of the family tree spreading over many generations. When Dad passed away at the age of 94, I am sad to say that none of us children were really into genealogy. I guess because I was the closest in proximity to his home, and I was willing to, I brought home bags and binders of information about both sides of the family. It was cool to find out that my mother was part of the Mayflower Society, being a direct descendant of one of her passengers.

At the age of 40, I felt a call that changed my life forever. I was working as a regional manager of a number of coffee shops. It was a well-paying position with many perks. It was on a Sunday evening that God made it clear He had something new for my life. The next morning, I went to work and was let go. After some deep conversations with my wife, it was clear that I was being called into the ministry. I headed back to school to earn my Bachelor's degree at the University of Connecticut. It was then time to determine where I would attend seminary. I opted for Southern Baptist Theological Seminary since they had an extension center in Northboro, Massachusetts. It took nearly eight years to earn my Master of Divinity Degree.

I was called to serve as the Pastor of First Congregational Church in Torrington in 2004. As I was setting up my office in my home, I stumbled upon the papers my father had left behind. Tucked inside an old brown binder, I found a plastic grocery bag that contained some ledgers from the early 1900s and what looked like old letters. There was currency from the Civil War era and other papers as well. I checked with my brother, a numismatist or a coin collector, and he was happy to take the currency. I took out one of the letters and carefully began to unfold it. It was there in my office, sitting at my desk, under a bright desk lamp, that two worlds collided. One by one, I opened the letters, being careful to treat them with respect and honor as my father would have. Each letter was handwritten, folded, and sealed with wax. No envelope protected them, and their storage container had been a plastic bag, yet here they were in amazing condition. Had there been letters between families living in the same town or even the same state, it would be hard to believe they still existed. Some of these letters had sailed across the Atlantic Ocean from Africa to the United States back in the 1840s. In my eyes, this was truly a miracle.

As I began to read these letters, I could see that God was bringing together two members of a family separated by over

170 years. It is in these letters that I was introduced to an amazing woman by the name of Ann L. Harnden, an ancestor I had never heard of before. The notation in one of the binders kept by my father simply read, "I was about to discover who this woman was and her journey of faith. The more I read, the more her story touched my heart. The extraordinary courage and fortitude she exhibited was an example of the power of the Holy Spirit that dwelt within her."

Her story had to be told. I could not let this opportunity slip away. It would take years before I could find the time and the opportunity to sit down and share her story with the world. Her love of God leaped from the pages of these letters. Her devotion to following Him resonated in my heart.

To leave family, home, and country in service to the Lord inspired within me a deeper devotion to following God wherever he called, including a mission trip to India where I learned only a bit of what it means to be a missionary in a foreign land in the 21st century, not the 19th century. In the Book of Esther in the Old Testament of the Bible, we read of a young woman who is chosen to bring salvation to her people. In Esther 4:14, we read, "For if you remain silent at this time, relief and deliverance for the Jews will arise from another place, but you and your father's family will perish. And who knows but that you have come to your royal position for such a time as this?"

God has a plan for your life. There are times when God will ask you to do things that are difficult. Can God accomplish His plans without you? Yes. But He asks you to participate in His plans because it strengthens your faith.

You may face uncertainty, failure, fear, and suffering as you try to fulfill God's plans for your life. But God is with you every step of the way. He is working all things for the good of those who love Him.

This verse was spoken to Esther because she found herself in a position to rescue her people, the Jews, from death. But, if she followed through with her plans to intervene, she put her own life at risk because of the laws at that time. Esther was reluctant, but she trusted that God sovereignly put her in that position at that time to do what needed to be done. This tested her faith, and God was working all things for good in her situation.

My prayer is that as you read this book, you will connect with Ann and her story of faith, love, and loss as I have. Through this book, may you discover the purpose for which God has created you. When you discover that purpose and dedicate yourself to following wherever God leads you, your life will never be the same.

Contents

Dedication i
Acknowledgements ii
About the Author iii
Preface iv
Chapter 1: The Calling 1
Chapter 2: On Our Way 29
Chapter 3: God with Us 50
Chapter 4: The Embrace 67
Chapter 5: Mission Begins 85
Chapter 6: Our Hope 107
Chapter 7: Pressing Forward 123
Chapter 8: Welcomed Home 141
Chapter 9: Quieted Shoes 156
Chapter 10: Seeds Sown 169
Chapter 11: Don't Plan for God 187
Introduction to Appendix 205

Chapter 1: The Calling

Sitting on the front porch of her family home, Ann Harnden felt a tug upon her heart that unmistakably came from the Lord. It was her routine to take a few minutes each morning to sit and read scriptures and pray. Today it felt different. It was as though God had chosen to speak to her in a deeper way — in a way that stirred deeply within her soul. Little did she know the path and purpose God had planned for her life, one that would stretch and strengthen her faith.

Miss Ann L. Harnden was always destined for great things under the shining and guiding light of the Lord. Her faith propelled her into a life of marvelous courage, hard sacrifice, intense devotion, and unending love that mirrored the life of our Savior, Jesus Christ. As a young, single woman in Haverhill, Massachusetts, in the United States, Ann's life was greatly influenced by the Evangelical Church that was active in her community and town.

She was guided by her faith, willing to accept the loving embrace of the Lord in his mercy, shining through her into the world and onto others. Her life was a testament to the endless capabilities and opportunities that are fulfilled when one opens one's heart up to the Lord; her experience is a lasting example of the glory, comfort, and love that one gains when one puts their fate into the hands of the Almighty. While remembering that He already set out the correct path for her and that all she needs to do is have the courage to walk on that path. She thought of the prophet Jeremiah and the words he wrote at the time of his calling. *"The word of the Lord came to me, saying, Before I formed you in the womb I knew you, before you were born I set you apart; I appointed you as a prophet to the nations."*

Alas, Sovereign Lord," I said, "I do not know how to speak; I am too young." But the Lord said to me, "Do not say, 'I am too young.' You must go to everyone I send you to and say whatever I command you. Do not be afraid of them, for I am with you and will rescue you," declares the Lord." Ann would go on to walk the path God set before her despite all restraints and fears.

As the 4th in line of eight children, Ann was entrusted with the responsibility of setting an example for her siblings. Her upbringing instilled a strong sense of familial duty and loyalty. The blue eyes and blonde hair she possessed were a feature that was seen in her entire family. They were all striking with their features and had average heights and weights. The family really looked like one unit when they walked together, and anyone could tell that they were related. Ann cherished her family bonds and deeply valued the relationships she shared with her parents and siblings. Her seven siblings all loved her, and she acted as a mother figure to the younger ones. This fostered in her a personality that was incredibly kind and nurturing; she was fiercely determined to give to others and make others feel comfortable and enlightened in God's Word. Raised in a household where faith and love prevailed, Ann's upbringing had a profound impact on her character. She was a deeply religious person and had a strong connection to the church and Jesus.

Additionally, while her mother was loving, she possessed a firm and stern demeanor, imparting important values and discipline to her children. Ann held her mother's guidance in high regard, viewing her as a source of wisdom and strength. Therefore, Ann was also resilient and passionate, ready to take on new and exciting opportunities.

Dr. Martyn, a resident of Haverhill, Massachusetts, approached Ann's mother about the possibility of Ann working for him. Upon her mother's approval, Ann moved away from her home and in with the Martyn family. There she earned for herself as she worked with Dr. Martyn and his family. She was also a ward in the home of the Martyn's. The Martyn family, devout Christians themselves, embraced Ann as one of their own. They had three children, two boys and a girl, ranging in age from 12 to 3 years old. The years spent with them shaped her understanding of love, happiness, and the importance of community. Within the Martyn household, Ann had found a sense of belonging, joy, and acceptance that nourished her soul. She joined them when they went to church and sat with them as they prayed. She took care of their children and helped around the house with chores and gatherings that took place there. The young girl, Ruth, needed some special care. She seemed to always struggle with her schoolwork and found it difficult to get along with other girls of her age. Ann became a source of peace and stability for Ruth. She helped her with her schoolwork and took time to show her how to make friends. She would often read the Bible to her at night and sing her lullabies.

Ann's deep-rooted religious faith and family-oriented nature defined her character. Her life was intertwined with her spiritual devotion and the love she held for her family. These foundational elements of her identity continued to play a vital role as she embarked on a journey that put her faith and resilience to the test.

Ann found that there were aspects of her life that weighed on her heart and caused her difficulty. Although she was blessed by the Lord in many ways, and her life had been rather uneventful, she wanted more out of life. She had dreams and hopes that a young lady of her era would often find unattainable or even unthinkable. At that time, there was great emphasis on marriage and domesticity: The prevailing belief in the 1840s was that a woman's primary role was to be a wife and mother. Young women were expected to prioritize marriage and prepare for their future domestic responsibilities instead of pursuing paid employment or a career. This was a time when the idea of "true womanhood" was prevalent, and virtues such as piety, purity, submissiveness, and domestic skills were the qualities that were most desired and ingrained into women from an early age. There were also significant restrictions on employment and therefore, opportunities for young women to pursue paid employment outside the home were limited. Women were often confined to traditionally female occupations such as teaching, domestic service, or working in textile mills. The prevailing belief was that a woman's place was in the home, and paid work was seen as secondary to her domestic duties.

As for Ann, she would have been trained in domestic duties and encouraged to find a husband and live her whole life caring for the household and her family. However, she was destined for far more than that, and God gave her the courage to seek more in her life. Due to this, she vowed that she would make her life meaningful and show that women, too, had a divine purpose and could handle responsibility, especially when it came to spreading God's message. For this reason, she participated in the church's work often, becoming a Sunday school teacher and helping organize events. She also excelled at her work with Dr. Martyn, which made him value her greatly.

Yet, Ann believed she was being called to more. She wanted to have a real mission and purpose in life that she could be proud of. Her desires came to fruition in her life, and they continued to inspire her future line as her descendants today continue to work for the Lord and are motivated by her story to push themselves in their own lives and follow the lessons they have learned from Ann L. Harnden. Due to Ann becoming acquainted with someone who saw her passion and love for the Lord, she would go on to have a great adventure that was blessed and dedicated to God and the spread of His Word.

By the grace of the Lord, Ann met Mr. William Raymond who would become a mentor and help her on her journey to attain fulfillment in her work for Christ. He, too, was a man of faith, having dedicated himself to the work of the Lord. It would take a leap of faith on his part to trust such an inexperienced young lady to join him and his family to become part of the biggest calling of his life. When they first met, Ann was teaching the littlest children in the church, sitting on the hardwood floor and reading from the Bible. She was telling them the story of Jesus' birth. She spoke with excitement and awe in her voice as she related the story of the angels coming to the shepherds in the field. Then when the scene shifted to the manger, she quietly whispered as if not to wake the baby Jesus. Her passion for children and the Word of God was a source of inspiration.

Mr. Raymond was an American Missionary who defied all norms and resisted any unethical or exploitative practices that did not align with the teachings of Jesus Christ: to "love thy neighbor as thyself." He focused on teaching and spreading the word of God to the African American people who resided in America at the time and later went on to preach on missionary journeys to the people of Africa under the Evangelical Missionary Society. Through their connection at the Evangelical church, Mr. Raymond played a significant role in Ann's life as he encouraged her to live out her trust in God, giving her opportunities and adventures that later became an integral part of her identity in Christ and came to define and strengthen her faith.

The tale of the courage, faith, and love of God that Miss Ann L. Harnden and Mr. William Raymond embarked upon is absolutely fascinating. Laden with spiritual meaning and promise that deserves to be told as a narrative, it inspires and fosters a deepening and strengthening of our faith in God and His miracles. This story takes place in the 1840s, as we begin in Massachusetts after Miss Ann and Mr. Raymond have already been acquainted through the church. In the 1840s in America, the effects of the transatlantic slave trade were still apparent and severe, with the Black people of America being grossly mistreated, underrepresented, and virtually banished from society. However, not all men were prejudiced and violent, and one such man was Mr. William Raymond.

He was a man of Christ, a teacher to the slaves, and a preacher of the Word of God. The man's engagements with social justice and resistance to oppressive structures were impressive and deserving of praise. He was born in the year 1815 and raised in Ashby, Massachusetts, where his family believed that he would grow up to one day become a mechanic. However, even as a boy, he felt a strong pull toward the Church and Christ, which compelled him to study the Bible and its teachings in depth to realize his personal convictions and beliefs.

As an adult, he studied at Amherst College but only spent two years there, given his dedication to justice and love went against the social norms of the time. He spent much of his hours at college teaching Black families and mingling with Black communities. This was seen in an extremely disapproving light by the authorities at his college, who took his actions as a violation of their ethical and moral code and used it as a justification to remove him from the institute. The last straw for the college administration was when he gave a black girl a ride back home after he saw her struggling to find transportation. This kind of conduct by administrations and structures of power was fairly common in the 1800s and was a phenomenon that was seen throughout the United States of America. In fact, all around the world, in countries that were ruled by the Whites. Mr. Raymond did, however, feel that the measures they took were uncalled for and unjustified as he had been a model student and a good member of his college society. Several of his teachers had also felt the same way, but he failed to convince the college authorities against his expulsion.

This caused him to move to Ohio, where he attended the Oberlin Collegiate and studied Theology and Classics. As his knowledge of the scriptures expanded his faith was deepened which inspired him to live the rest of his life as a minister and a missionary in the Evangelical Church. He received his license to preach and, shortly after, moved to Canada to begin his journey with the Church.

In Canada, he mainly worked with and lived with fugitive slaves and people of color. To them, he preached the Word of God and exposed them to the teachings of Christ. Throughout his time teaching and preaching to slaves in Canada, Mr. Raymond worked to help them raise funds so they could travel to Africa—the homeland they originated from. Due to his deep desire to spread the Word of God, he wished to see the people he taught also share his devotion and carry on his and the Church's teachings to the brethren. It was through this work that William, his wife Eliza, and Ann began partnering in ministry, as they all had a passion for teaching and a deep faith in the Word of God.

While Mr. Raymond was still in Massachusetts, Ann regularly attended the Evangelical Church, where he was a minister. His sermons on Sunday touched her heart, and soon it became apparent that Mr. Raymond was a man of great faith, love, and kindness. He would, many years later, inform Ann about the Mende Mission that was being carried out by the Evangelical Mission Society and tell her that she could potentially have the opportunity to join the mission if she were given permission from the society.

Ann was overjoyed and began working toward joining the mission, spreading God's Holy Word. She knew of the missions that churches all over America had been carrying out and was overjoyed that now, women, too, were playing a big part in them, even embarking on treacherous journeys and visiting strange, unknown lands. There were many

Christian missionary missions to various regions, including but not limited to India, China, Canada, Australia, West Africa, South Africa, and Japan. They worked to spread God's truth and allow people from all corners of the world to be exposed to Christianity. Along the way, they carried out a lot of good work, spreading Christ's teachings of love, harmony, peace, and sacrifice.

The motive behind some of these missions, when seen historically and from a modern-day perspective, is contentious and requires one to have a good knowledge of the context and ideology of the time to comprehend it in a critical manner. While the mission to spread God's Word is Holy and righteous, some men who were seeking profits, land, and power used it as a way to spread their power over the world and slowly take over other nations.

Many justified slavery while it was still rampant by saying that it was a way to bring people onto the correct religious path; while this could have potentially been an honorable and spiritually correct idea, the ways in which it was carried out went against the teachings of God as people of color were often oppressed.

But things got better, as we see in the case of Ann, Mr. and Mrs. Raymond, and others, who worked with the Church and Mission Society to help better the lives of underprivileged communities in America and around the world. Ann and the Raymonds stayed in contact after their encounters in the Church; they communicated through letters as Mr. Raymond went on and preached abroad in Canada. When he returned to the United States in the early 1840s, he told Ann about the mission he planned to go on to Mende land (present-day Sierra Leone). What Mr. Raymond desired was to begin and lead his very own mission under the guiding light of Christ and with direction and permission from the Evangelical Church.

He wanted to educate and preach to the people of West Africa by opening up a Church and a school there. This desire had been solidified and became a goal that had to be achieved in his mind as his work with the Black communities in America showed him how the people struggled and how desperately they needed the comfort and peace that could only be achieved through faith in God and Jesus Christ.

While these plans were brewing in William's mind, God worked in his glory and enabled him to act on the calling that was tugging on his heart and soul. This was because, in 1841, the Supreme Court of the United States of America ruled a verdict that said the Amistad Africans were now free.

These Africans were people who had been forced into slavery and revolted against their freedom being taken away by force. They had successfully taken their freedom and rebelled against their slave owners by organizing a revolt. The story is a fascinating historical event that captures the grace and power of God and reveals how His plans for people are predetermined and laid out so that they may work in His glory. In 1839, Portuguese slave hunters went to Mende land and abducted a great many West African people. They were taken so that they could become slaves in Cuba, which at the time was a Spanish colony.

The people had been taken by force, and great violence was inflicted upon them. The whole ordeal was also illegal as slavery had been abolished, and the hundreds of Africans who were taken were becoming part of an illegal and illegitimate Atlantic slave trade despite slavery being outlawed by countries like the United States, Britain, and Spain.

Spanish plantation owners Jose Ruiz and Pedro Montes purchased 53 of these people and took them on a ship called the Amistad. They set sail from Havana, which was a bustling slave trade hub at the time, and set sail for Puerto Principe. The two buyers had plantations there, and they wanted slaves to work on them.

Some days passed with the ship traveling the treacherous waters and transporting its cargo of illegal captives a quarter way across the world, ripping them out of their homes and making their lives into a living hell. This was until one of the captives named, Sengbe Pieh, was able to unshackle himself; perhaps Sengbe had been working through the Lord and had been influenced by his to pluck up the courage to fight against the violence being inflicted upon him. He freed himself and proceeded to unshackle the rest of his fellow captives so they could organize themselves and plan a collective revolt against their Spanish captors. The newly formed group proceeded to arm themselves with knives, pieces of wood, legs of chairs, and the very chains that held them hostage. Using these, they took the ship and killed the captain. Interestingly they also killed the cook who was aboard the ship as the man had taunted the captives saying that once they reached their destination, he would butcher them and turn them into meals for the people on the plantation.

The group then made the two slave traders turn the ship and change the course of travel so that they may return to where they came from—the Mende land. However, the two slave traders managed to change the course of the ship during the darkness of night and trick the captives into believing they were headed to West Africa when in reality, they were going toward the United States. Once the ship entered the US Naval territory, the US brig Washington found the ship, bordered it, and held the captives on board. They charged them as captives with mutiny and claimed salvage rights over them. The Africans were charged with murder and piracy and were imprisoned in Connecticut. These charges were dropped, but the African people remained imprisoned for two years while the court decided what to do with them and who had rights to them.

In February 1841, John Quincy Adams argued the Mende were free men illegally captured and sold into slavery and, as such, should be returned to Africa. After the Supreme Court ruled in favor of the captives, Adams wrote his co-counsel, Roger Sherman Baldwin, saying,

"The decision of the Supreme Court in the case of the Amistad has this moment been delivered by Judge Story. The captives are free...Yours in great haste and great joy."

In November 1841, the Mende Africans gave Adams a Bible as a token of their gratitude. An accompanying letter stated:

To The Honorable John Quincy Adams.

Most Respected Sir,

The Mendi People give you thanks for all your kindness to them. They will never forget your defense of their rights before the Great Court at Washington. They feel that they owe to you, in a large measure, their deliverance from the Spaniards, and from Slavery or Death. They will pray for you, Mr. Adams, as long as they live. May God bless and reward you!

We are about to go home to Africa. We go to Sierra Leone first, and there we reach Mendi very quick. Good missionary men will go with us. It has been a precious book to us in prison, and we love to read it know we are free. Mr. Adams, we want to make you a present of a beautiful Bible. Will you

please accept it, and when you look at it or read it, remember your poor and grateful clients! We read in this holy book, "If it had not been the Lord who was on our side, when men rose up against us, then they had swallowed us up quick when their wrath was kindled against us.... Blessed be the Lord, who hath not given us a prey to their teeth. Our soul is escaped as a bird out of the snare of the fowlers: the snare is broken, and we are escaped. Our help is in the name of the Lord, who made heaven and earth. Psalm CXXIV.

For the Mendi People,

Cinque Kinna Kale

Boston, Nov. 6th. 1841

To this, John Quincy Adams replied,

Lewis Tappan, Esq. New York

Dear Sir,

--I received and accept with thanks the elegant Bible, presented to me by Cinque, Kinna, Kale, and the thirty-two other Mendians, who are indebted to you, and your benevolent associates, probably for their lives, certainly for their deliverance from unjust prosecution, and long protracted imprisonment and finally for the means of returning to their own country....[I] hope for the consummation of your kindness to them in the accomplishment of their restoration in freedom and safety to their native land. I am, with great respect, dear sir, faithfully yours, JOHN QUINCY ADAMS

Adam's efforts were monumental for the people of Amistad; however, the courts did not provide funds for their return, and thus, these people came into contact with missionary societies that were raising funds to get slaves and captured Africans back to their home nations. One of these was the Evangelical Mission Society, where Mr. Raymond was a member.

The society founded a committee called the Amistad Committee for this task and appointed Mr. Raymond as a teacher for the Amistad people so he could work for their protection and welfare. Thus, Mr. Raymond traveled to Farmington, Connecticut, to be a part of this Holy practice that protected God's children in their time of suffering and hardship. In the beginning, the plan was to have the Amistad people return to their nation to be reunited with their land, people, and culture.

The hand of the Lord is apparent as he worked to realize the dreams of Mr. Raymond along with the need of the freed Amistad captives. His grace and mercy shone upon all the people involved as He guided and aided them on a path that would benefit them and keep them in loving peace and comfort.

When Mr. Raymond realized that a mission would certainly be making the arduous journey to West Africa, he informed Ann about it and urged her to travel with him, his wife and children and other missionaries to Mende land so she may embrace the word and work of the missionaries and continue practicing her faith by teaching the Mende people what she had learned about God's Word in America. By this time, Ann had given her life to the work of Jesus Christ and was working with freed captives to teach them and care for them.

Her upbringing in Haverhill and exposure to anti-abolitionist movements and collectives instilled in her a passion for social justice and the advocating for equality through the spread of God's Word.

Mr. Raymond knew of a vessel that was going to leave New York for the mission and was mentally preparing Ann for the journey.

The arrangements would take some time. He would have to speak to Mr. Tappan, who was organizing the mission, and he would need permission from the Evangelical Mission Society to have Ann accompany them. Mr. Raymond, William, would be traveling with his wife, Eliza.

He told Ann that he wished for her to join him on his mission, where he would set up a church and school in Mende. All of this would be completely new to the region, so they would be starting their work from scratch. Mr. Raymond warned Ann about how difficult the mission would be and how it would test her faith, resilience, and her devotion. It would be an endeavor that would affect her body, mind, and spirit. In his letter telling her about the opportunity, Mr. Raymond said:

"But my dear sister, have you fully counted the cost? It is no small thing to be a missionary. The responsibility Oh how awful! Then you have got to leave that dear mother of yours behind – never to hear her kind voice again till it is turned to an angel's. Those brothers and sisters can you say good-bye? Then there are all your Christian friends.

There are all the comforts not to say luxuries of civilization. There is a prospect of living while you do, live a single life, have you thought of that? There is a prospect of sickness, amongst strangers amongst heathen – perhaps death. Have you counted the cost? You will have trials that you now cannot conceive of? You must find the witness that God has called you continually."

– Extract from a letter from Wm Raymond to Miss Ann L. Harnden, dated October 5th, 1843

He highlighted how Ann would be leaving behind the only home she had known and how she may not feel comfortable in a new land with new people. Yet, he was also extremely encouraging and urged her to speak with her mother on the matter.

He also consoled her in his letters, saying that all her needs would be seen to with the funding from the Evangelical Mission Society, and he reminded her that God would be with her every step of the way. He was especially adamant that she joined since his own brother, who was in Canada at the time, could not join him on their journey.

This news gave Ann much to reflect on as she considered the journey.

There would be adventure and excitement. There would be challenges and dangers. It seemed to be the opportunity she was waiting for. She was so young, in her early twenties, new to the work God had called her to.

She thought back to that day she was sitting on the porch and the deep sense she had that God was calling her to a deeper faith and trust in Him.

She believed God had brought her to this point and was testing her faith. But the calling burned in her heart, and to help her make a decision regarding it, she decided that she would speak with her mother.

Ann would spend hours in her room praying and seeking God's wisdom and direction. Her desire to reach the lost and now the opportunity to spread God's Word in Africa was fueled by the abolitionist movement of the early 1800s.Haverhill, Massachusetts, was a community that sought to abolish slavery.

The Evangelical Church, where the Martyns and the Harndens were members of a Black-friendly church. For the most part, the Black people there were relatively well treated. Of course, the intricacies of racism and the ways it can present even in good people must be accounted for.

Even the people of Haverhill could not completely erase the ideology that had been drilled into them for centuries, and at times, they fell short.

Yet, this did not stop the abolitionists from continuing to move their cause forward. In August of 1836, the Reverend David Root delivered a sermon before the Anti-Slavery Society of Haverhill, Massachusetts. He spoke about the unyielding grip of the oppressors of the Black people. He believed that God would be a witness against their actions. The time was coming when the merchandise of men's souls would cease. He quoted from Revelation 18:11,

"And the merchants of the earth shall weep and mourn over her; for no man buyeth her merchandize anymore; -the merchandize of beasts and sheep and horses and chariots and slaves and souls of men."

His desire echoed the desire of the Abolitionist Society to see slavery become extinct throughout this nation and the world.

He looked forward to the day when there will be a great celebration when no man shall enslave his fellow man, and we shall all experience our sacred right to freedom.

This is the atmosphere in which Ann was raised in Haverhill.

She stayed with the Martyn family, who took her under their wing as she was a part of the Church they went to. At the house, she worked as a maid and a nanny, taking care of the Martyn children, cooking and cleaning for the family, and assisting them with other tasks and chores around the household.

The Martin family was abolitionist, so open thinking and desire for a fairer society rubbed off on Ann. The role that the Church played in the relationship between the Martyns and Ann cannot be understated, as the two parties would go together to attend Church.

At the Church, the Martyn's, a white family, and Ann mingled with and taught the Black church members, and so the entire Church community saw themselves as one and the same, just as the Lord sees all of his people as one united family under the Lordship of Jesus.

In the 1840s, the role of the Church in the lives of the people was great and extremely important. Church and family were inseparable as the Church grounds, events, and services were always a family and community gathering ordeal. People would go for service more than three times a week—on Wednesdays, Fridays, and Sundays.

There they would meet new people, establish meaningful and fulfilling relationships, and carry on the work of God. They would use the Church for all aspects of their lives. If the heat was not working, the Church would give them shelter. If they needed a friend to talk to and guide them, they went to the ministers. If they needed a space to have a fundraising event, the Church was the go-to spot. The entire life of the Christian people of the time was intrinsically connected to the Church. Ann and the Martyns were also connected because of their shared faith in Christ and their devotion to the Church.

Ann had been part of this Church since her childhood; she had gone to Sunday school there, been a part of the choir, and been there for every Christmas, Easter, and Good Friday. Church was where she grew up. She later went on to give back to the Church by becoming a Sunday school teacher there. She had been truly blessed to be residing in Haverhill and going to the local Church there.

The Martyns had taken Ann in so that her mother may care for her other siblings, seven in all, while Ann found her place in the world and earned her own money. Although she was a ward of the Martins, Ann felt like family and enjoyed years of happiness, joy, and love with a devout Christian family surrounding her.

She thought about all of this and how comfortable she now felt with her situation when considering the mission to Mende. She struggled with the fact that she would now have to leave it all behind and leave the people she loved and who loved her. She especially thought about her mother. Talking to her mother about the mission could help ease Ann's fears but bringing up the topic terrified her.

She and her mother were extremely close, and Ann did not want to leave her alone in the country, especially since she had always been her confidant, most cherished friend, and comforter.

Ann feared that her mother would believe she was abandoning all that had made her who she was if she decided to go on the mission, but she would not leave without her mother's blessing.

For the most part, Ann was well taken care of; she did not have to struggle while caring for the Martyn family. Her work outside the home was mostly with the community she had become so familiar with. They would be kind to her, give her chances, and help if she lacked in any area. If she were to go to Mende, she would be doing far more serious and official work, and she would be watched by Mr. William Raymond and the Evangelical Missionary Society.

She would have to prove herself to them and the people to whom she would be spreading the message. Ann knew that women in 1840 were not typically considered active members of society who would work outside of the home; they were expected to be subordinates, occupy lower positions in power structures, and depend on the men in their lives. If Ann went on this mission, she would be given responsibility like never before; she would have to prove that women, too, could handle and excel at such arduous tasks. All night Ann prayed about the mission, filled with emotions such as fear, excitement, dread, discomfort, and joy; throughout it, she remembered the Father and the Son, hoping they would guide her and tell her the right thing to do.

She prayed to the Lord that He would grant her courage and strength to complete the journey and that He would keep her safe and healthy during her travels. Then, she went on her way to talk to her mother.

They sat in the front room of Ann's family home. It took courage and a deep faith in God to start the conversation. The young children had been put to bed, so they were alone. Ann sat on the settee next to her mother. Her knee bounced up and down with excitement and trepidation. She looked at her mother and told her about the letter and God's call to the holy mission. The first thing her mother said in response to Ann's request was a moment that became seared into her mind.

The words *"I would rather follow you to the grave than see you go to Africa."* had been said with such fear and overwhelming sadness that Ann had almost abandoned all her hopes and dreams right then. But the power of the Lord flowed through her and enabled her to find the correct words in response.

Ann told her mother:

"I will not be like the wife of Lot. I will not look back when God has given me instruction and set out a path before me. This is my calling, Mother; this is the plan that He has written for me. I am to become a missionary and speak His word in His Holy name. I know that this is what I was always meant to do. I must follow the command of God and be His pride. In doing so, I will also become your pride."

Reference from a lost letter from Ann to her mother, dated *November 1843*

These words touched Ann's mother, who begrudgingly decided to let her daughter become a missionary who would spread the message of faith. She saw that her daughter understood the cost and what she would be giving up if she left. She knew Ann's heart and life now belonged to the Lord and the Church and that she would have to sacrifice her daughter to achieve a sense of fulfillment and be at peace spiritually. Through their long, tear-filled conversation, Ann's mother saw that the responsibility of this mission weighed on the shoulders of her daughter, who remained bravely determined and solid in her faith.

She knew that Ann knew that this was her purpose. She knew that her own test was to sacrifice her daughter, risk her being lost at sea, and risk not knowing about her status for months at a time. It devastated her and broke her heart to pieces, but she knew that if she did not agree and let Ann go, she would be going against the will of God and causing her child a great deal of suffering.

Though a battle raged in her heart and mind, she gave Ann her blessing and wished for her safety and for God to be with her wherever she went.

Once Ann left her home, her mother wept. She was afraid she would never see her child again and that she was going to now start a life of great struggle and pain, all without the comfort of motherly advice or a hug from the one who held her for nine months in her womb. She never really wanted to let Ann go; she never wanted to feel this alone; she never wanted her child to suffer and face hardships.

However, she was also extremely proud of Ann and her courage. She was proud that her daughter could do incredible work for the Lord despite being a single woman.

Her daughter had rarely left the comforts of the town she grew up in. Mrs. Harnden's head hurt, and her heart cried out each time she thought about her daughter on a dangerous ship and then in a strange land, but she did let her go and prayed every night after that for her safety.

She prayed that God would be with her daughter and that the Holy Spirit would flow through her and aid her as she taught and preached in the heat and suffering of West Africa. Ann's mother assumed that the tribes in Mende would be warring and that one of the mission's goals was to help stop the conflict.

She feared that Ann would get injured while trying to do this work, so she also prayed to the Lord that the battles in Mende would cease through the grace and tolerance that would be spread to the people by the mission.

A few days after this, a letter from Mr. Raymond arrived at Haverhill and found its way into the hands of Miss Ann L. Harnden, who opened it with her hands shaking and her heart pounding. It said:

"Dear Sis Ann,

Yours of the 29th that I received last night. I also received a letter from Br. Tappan in which he says, "Last evening, the committee met and had a long session.

Your letter was read. Also, Miss Harnden's. The committee decided it is best for you, Mrs. Raymond, and Miss H. to leave for Africa this fall." Thus, you see it is decided by the com that you are to go. He says, "I will inform you as soon as I can when the vessel will sail for Sierra Leone." You see, the Lord has opened the way for you to go – has given you favor in the eyes of the Comm. Is not this wonderful?

- Extract from a letter from Wm Raymond to Miss Ann L. Harnden, dated October 5th, 1843

It was indeed wonderful, and it lifted her spirits. She would be leaving soon; she would become a missionary working in Mende, Africa, as part of a team that would be the first ever in the region. She was going to teach, educate, and preach. She was going to help fulfill the vision and mission of the missionaries—to have the Gospel of the Lord be heard, to Baptize people, and to have the Holy Spirit work through them as they spread the teachings of Christ.

Chapter 2: On Our Way

On October 5, 1841, Mr. Lewis Tappan, who was leading and organizing this mission to Mende, sent a letter to Ann Harnden of Haverhill, Massachusetts, confirming that she would be part of the Mende Mission if she desired.

As soon as Ann saw that the letter had come from New York, she knew what the topic of discussion in the writing would be. She was filled with nervous energy, and her hands shook as she opened the letter. It read:

Dear Friend,

Mr. and Mrs. Raymond are very desirous that you should accompany them to Africa to assist in their labors on behalf of the Mendi Mission and it appears by your letter to Mr. Raymond, dated August 6th which he put into my hands, that you are very desirous of going. The executive committee of the Union Missionary Society has determined on accepting your proposition and to aid you in your benevolent enterprise. They wish you health, the opportunity of doing good in the vineyard of the Lord and the grace and blessing of the Lord of the vineyard.

Very truly and sincerely yours,

Louis Tappan

Corresponding Secretary

Upon reading the content of the letter, Ann was overjoyed and knelt down to thank the Lord for looking down upon her and enabling her to act on her dreams and desires. She was grateful for the trust and love that Mr. and Mrs. Raymond had in her, and she was looking forward to spending time with them and their children while they embarked on a holy and noble quest for the Lord and his Gospel.

It had also filled her with a thrill to know that Mr. Louis Tappan had deemed her worthy of such a difficult and glorious undertaking as she had much admiration for the man who had solidified his name in history and worked for years to further the goals of the missionaries. He was a man who had accomplished much as God's light shone through him and as Jesus' teachings guided his every move.

Louis Tappan was a resident of Massachusetts. Born in 1788, he was the man that the region needed during the post-slavery era and the abolitionist movement, as much of his work was geared toward these and the Church.

In addition to being a philanthropist and abolitionist, he was a merchant and industrialist. So he managed to accumulate a fortune, a substantial chunk of which he used to fund Church missions and other projects that were geared toward ending slavery. He was considered a pioneer in the areas that he chose to work within, and he was a prominent figure in the attempts to support and facilitate African people who wished to go back to their home countries. Tappan was a deeply pious man who was invested in the life of the Evangelical Church and applied what he learned in Church to his life, social work, and business. Through the grace of our ever-loving and benevolent Lord, his economic endeavors flourished, enabling him to fund many projects that aligned with his Christian views and his view of how Americans should function as a society.

In fact, he was one of the many figures who funded the mission that Ann was to embark upon, and so, to hear from such an influential and important man was something glorious and special for Ann, who lived a simple life in a small town.

She had heard of how this brilliant man had funded the American Anti-Slavery Society and established the Oberlin College, where both Black and White students studied together. He also played a significant role in the freeing of the Amistad people who were going to be with Ann on the ship to Mende land. John Quincy Adams, the sixth President of the United States of America, had even stated that Louis Tappan was the most significant figure who played a role in and enabled the freedom of the Amistad Africans. Once the men had reached the port, the abolitionists who heard of the incident contacted Louis Tappan, knowing of his unwavering devotion to the anti-slavery cause. He was extremely dedicated and passionate about this case and provided top-notch legal representation to the Amistad men. He also raised money for their defense and cultivated public support for their case. He formed the 'Amistad Committee' that provided this legal aid; this was the space where decisions regarding the litigation were made.

They were the ones who filed the civil lawsuit against Ruiz and Montes, focusing on the battery, assault, and false imprisonment that the group had endured. Once they were freed (the credit for this largely went to Tappan), he worked with the Evangelical Mission Society to transport them back to their homes and along the way as the society set up a mission there.

Ann greatly admired him and was excited to work with him. She had also heard of all the violence, pushback, and hardships he had to go through to further his personal mission, which was birthed out of his love for God and God's creation. The stories of what he went through due to his zeal and beliefs sent a chill through Ann.

Louis and his brother Arthur Tappan had accrued much resentment and hate from groups who had opposing beliefs to theirs, especially in the pro-slavery states. This caused them to suffer attacks from mobs and terrorists who targeted them and tried to make them abandon their cause through violence. Since the Tappans had dedicated themselves to serving God, they were blessed by His faithful protection and provision. Unscathed and undeterred, these attacks only fueled their desire to serve God and fulfill their mission. One incident that was particularly violent and surprising was when a mob broke into Louis's home during a meeting. They stole his furniture, threw it into a pile on the street, and burned it all in a gesture that was exceedingly violent and violated the privacy and sanctity of the home. He was followed by this kind of violence throughout his life but due to his conviction and trust in the Lord God he continued his work. Ann believed that she could also have the same kind of trust and confidence that Mr. Louis Tappan had in God and His gentle mercy. She fortified herself, holding onto his stories for inspiration and proof that God would keep her safe, too, as she worked in His name and for His glory. With this strong feeling of hope and trust in her heart, Ann confirmed her acceptance of the invitation to join the Mende Mission. In the following weeks of preparation, she spent much time with her beloved mother and Mr. and Mrs. Raymond along with their children. Ann was fond of the Raymond children, having formed a close relationship with them due to her work with the church, as she had taught all the children in Sunday school. They had also grown attached to her and viewed her as a mentor and an example of how to lead a good Christian life where Christ and the Church were central aspects of character. Ann was well-acquainted with Mrs. Raymond, who frequented the Church and spoke of her husband's endeavors with the abolitionist and missionary movements while he was away from his hometown.

She was excited to get closer to this marvelous young woman who supported her husband in his ministry. Ann and

Mrs. Raymond had also worked together on several occasions for church-related projects and gatherings where the women would often contribute by baking, cooking, and organizing the decor for Church meetings and occasions. Mrs. Raymond's oatmeal and raisin cookies were something that Ann always looked forward to and considered a delicacy.

(Here is the recipe that may have been passed down along the Raymond family line. I have no proof of this but I am putting it in, they are delicious.

Ingredients:

- *1 cup of flour*
- *1 cup of granulated sugar*
- *2 cups oatmeal*
- *1 ¼ cup of raisins*
- *1 cup butter*
- *3 eggs*
- *½ teaspoon salt*
- *¾ teaspoon baking soda*
- *2 teaspoons of cinnamon*

Cream together the butter and sugar, add beaten eggs. Mix together the flour, oatmeal, raisins, cinnamon, baking soda and salt. Add the dry mixture to the creamed mixture. This will make a stiff batter. Bake on a tin in the oven. No time or temperature was given. You would need to figure that out for yourself.)

They had also had some lengthy discussions about their beliefs in God and their disdain for the pro-slavery movements and practices that had plagued the land and caused so many good people a great amount of distress and suffering.

In addition, their friendship had further convinced Ann that she, too, wanted to be a missionary and dedicate her life to the spread of the Word of God. As Mrs. Raymond was older and wiser, Ann looked toward her for guidance and admired her for her dedication.

They would be together during their voyage and mission in the new land, and Ann felt a sense of comfort knowing that familiar faces would be mixed in with all the unfamiliar ones she would now soon be encountering. Mrs. Raymond was comforted by the same notion. She was weary about the fact that she was leaving the hometown she had always known, the one her children had grown up in and the one where she met her husband. She was accustomed to Massachusetts, aware of its working and entrenched in its social and religious community. She had sunk in her roots there, but now, she was about to leave it all behind and traverse the grand Atlantic Ocean with her children to a land unknown.

She had fought and advocated for Ann's inclusion on the mission as she knew that her children loved Ann and would feel extremely comfortable and safe in her presence. Having someone else from her own community and Church on the mission with her was something that Mrs. Raymond deeply desired, and now, she was extremely grateful that Ann would be joining.

She also knew that Ann was a young and healthy girl, and she was assured that any trouble that she might have during the voyage would be lessened with Ann's help, particularly when it came to the children and their well-being.

During preparation, the two women often visited each other and exchanged advice on what to carry along for the journey. They prayed together often, asking God to watch over them as they traveled, and they also prayed for the well-being of the people they were about to leave behind. Ann's mother would often join them during these prayers, crying and hugging her daughter once prayers were done. In the winter of 1841, the ship to Mende was set to depart. Ann traveled with the Raymond family to New York, where the ship was docked and where she would forever say goodbye to American soil. Her mother had sought to join her in New York, but her health had prevented her from doing so.

On her departure from their family home, Ann met her siblings and made them promise to take care of their mother while she was away. They also prayed together and had a grand family feast just before Ann left for New York, headed toward the home of Mr. Louis Tappan.

Once they arrived at his home, Ann wondered at the splendor of his home. Mr. Tappan had faced many trials and difficult times through the years but this home was proof that God had protected and provided for him. He was ever grateful to God for the blessings he had received.

Through these blessings he was able to do so much for the abolitionist movement. At his home, she dined and slept in peace and tranquility, served by his house staff. She also got to meet the famous Mr. Tappan, who had become something of a hero in her mind, and gained much knowledge and wisdom from conversing with him and hearing his speeches on the matters of the mission and his past work with the Church.

After a couple of nights, the guests at Mr. Tappan's home were invited to the Church for a public meeting that occurred a day before their departure. The ship they were about to make their home for the next several weeks was a brig named Frances Lord. The vessel's staff and captain had confirmed Saturday at 2 o'clock in the afternoon as the time that the missionaries would depart for Mende, and now, everyone was filled with excitement at the prospect. The gathering at the Church was held in celebration, devotion, and hope for a safe journey.

At the congregational space, the Raymond family and Ann made many new friends and acquaintances who wished them well and gave them their blessings. The public meeting was fruitful and informative, with the whole church getting the details of the mission and many contributing toward it with cash donations as well as the offering of supplies and food.

At the end of the meeting, the people who were soon to board the brig Frances Lord were beckoned toward the pulpit, where the congregation joined them and held their hands.

The group stood in a large circle and prayed to the Lord for wisdom, grace, and mercy. They prayed to the Holy Spirit, asking him to fill the missionaries with the courage and power to persist on their journey, and they prayed to Christ, the redeemer, to keep the missionaries safe. Deacon Ebenezer led the prayer.

Heavenly Father,

As we gather here tonight on the eve of their departure on this perilous journey to Mende, we humbly seek Your divine guidance and protection for our missionaries. Grant them courage in the face of unknown challenges, fortitude to endure hardships, and persistence to overcome obstacles on their path.

Watch over them as they navigate treacherous waters, and shield them from the storms that may threaten their course. May Your light shine upon them, illuminating their way and filling their hearts with unwavering faith.

Bless their efforts to spread Your message of love and hope among the people of Mende. Grant them the strength to persevere in their mission, even when faced with adversity. Lord, be their constant companion, offering solace in moments of doubt and providing reassurance in times of fear. May Your protective hand be upon them, keeping them safe from harm.

In Your name, we pray for each one of them and entrust them to Your care. Amen.

The sight was one to behold, with the entire community joined together in a passionate and faithful celebration to display their faith and love of God, supporting and encouraging the missionaries. All the sisters in Christ who were present at the meeting gave Ann and Mrs. Raymond a parting kiss along with their blessings. A few even gave them small gifts and trinkets to take with them on their voyage. Ann left the Church with a beautiful brooch shaped like a robin pinned to her collar—a reminder that the people back home supported, loved, and cherished her and her mission.

The next morning, Ann woke with a knot in the pit in her stomach, but at the same time, her heart and head were light and joyful. She had a hearty meal and packed her belongings. Then, just before noon, she, the Raymonds, and Mr. Tappan departed, and the group traveled half a mile north of the city in the North River up to Sandy Hook port.

The bustling port surrounding Ann was well alive with the hustle and bustle of sailors and cargo. The brig Frances Lord, stood tall with its sails neatly furled, ready to catch the wind and set them on their course. It was docked in the deep waters, which confused Ann as she did not yet know that smaller row boats would be transporting them to the deck of the ship. The group met with Captain Brown, who was in charge of getting them across the Atlantic safely. He was an experienced brig captain who told the group that he had sailed across the Atlantic more than thirty times already. He also introduced his crew that would be working on the brig, serving the missionaries for the coming months. These were the people who they would be interacting with for the next 58 days while on board. Ann was part of the first group that went aboard the brig. She stepped onto the worn deck, her eyes wide with excitement and a hint of nervousness as she had never before been aboard a sea vessel and certainly never one as massive as the Frances Lord. The newness of the experience filled her with anticipation and joy as she struggled to stay upright, becoming dizzy from the waves of the ocean. As a young, unmarried woman living in the mid-1800s, she had only dreamed of being a part of such a great adventure as this.

As she watched the crew scurrying about on the deck of the giant sailing vessel, Ann marveled at their efficiency and purpose. They seemed so familiar with the brig and its mechanisms, moving effortlessly across the deck and attending to their duties. They pulled ropes, scrubbed floors, and pulled up anchors as if they had been living on a brig since the day they were born. Their weathered faces and calloused hands spoke of countless journeys across the Atlantic.

The deck beneath Ann's feet felt slightly uneven, the worn wooden planks showing signs of age and countless footsteps that had come before hers. She took a moment to adjust to the gentle rocking motion of the brig, a sensation she had never experienced before. The rhythm of the waves beneath the planks reminded her that she was embarking on a journey far beyond her familiar shores. Excitement bubbled within her as she cast her gaze out to the horizon. The vast expanse of the ocean stretched before her, endless and mysterious. Ann imagined the sparkling waves beckoning her forward, promising new encounters and unforgettable experiences. She couldn't help but smile at the thought of the adventures that awaited her on another shore of the vast blue expanse.

Looking up, Ann marveled at the brig's rigging, a labyrinth of ropes and pulleys that seemed to connect the heavens with the deck below. She watched as the crew climbed the mast with practiced ease. The sails, neatly folded, awaited their time to unfurl and catch the wind, propelling them on their journey. The sound of the captain's voice barking orders, the creaking of the rigging, and the flapping of the sails all blended together into a symphony of anticipation. Ann couldn't help but feel a sense of privilege to be part of this grand adventure, to share her faith and bring hope to those in a distant land.

Soon, the rest of the missionaries joined her and prayed together one last time for safe passage. Mr. Tappan assured Ann that he would keep her mother informed about the whereabouts of the brig and the status of its passengers. She gave him a few details to add to his letter to her mother regarding the new things she had seen in the port, and he obliged. Then, they set sail. Ann was so excited that she stayed up on the deck for an hour, watching the crew work, the wind blowing through the sails and the ocean thrashing.

With every passing minute, the shore grew smaller, the familiar sights and sounds fading into the distance. Ann closed her eyes for a moment, allowing herself to fully immerse in the exhilaration of the moment. The vessel, carrying her and her fellow missionaries, sailed steadily toward the unknown, guided by a combination of faith and the skill of the crew.

As the Frances Lord sailed further into the Atlantic, Ann couldn't help but reflect on the enormity of the task ahead. She knew the road would not always be smooth, that challenges and uncertainties would surely arise. But she was filled with a deep conviction that she was exactly where she was meant to be, embracing the unknown with courage and determination while the light of God shone upon her and lived in her heart. In that moment, as the brig sailed on, Ann's heart was filled with a profound sense of gratitude and awe. She had embarked on a voyage that would test her faith, challenge her assumptions, and forever shape her perspective on the world. With each passing wave, she eagerly anticipated the adventures, friendships, and transformation that awaited her on the distant shores of Mende land to spread the Word of God. Later, Ann made her way through the brig, exploring the deck. Numerous supplies had been loaded there, all having been provided by the Evangelical Mission Society, Mr. Tappan, and other donors.

Aboard, there were meats, cheeses, grain, water, beans, and even some chickens and goats which would be used for their eggs, milk, and meat. Along with this, they had brought along medical supplies, navigation equipment, tools, fuel for the burners and lamps, and personal belongings. Ann was told that Mende would be extremely hot, so she donated most of her heavy sweaters and blankets to charity. This brig would be her home for the next 58 or so days, and so far, she was loving it. She made her way to her personal chambers that were located below deck. Her room was right opposite that of Mr. and Mrs. Raymond.

While the vessel was not luxurious, it was comfortable and kept in a neat condition. Ann's room was slightly small but designed to maximize comfort within the constraints of the brig. The walls were made of sturdy wood, giving the room a cozy and secure feel that made Ann feel comforted. A small porthole allowed a glimpse of the outside world and let in a stream of natural light during the day. Ann peeked through it to be greeted by the vastness of the blue ocean, stretched out until the horizon. Below the porthole was a single bed adorned with clean linens and a comfortable mattress; it was just as comfortable as the bed Ann had back at home. A simple wooden nightstand stood beside the bed, with a small oil lamp placed on top of it to be used after dark. Ann took out her Bible and placed it near the lamp as she would use its glow to read the scriptures later that night. At the foot of the bed was a large trunk that was to serve as the storage space for her clothes and other belongings. Against the wall, there was a compact writing desk. This excited her as she had brought with her papers and quills so that she may write down and document her journey. The desk featured a small inkwell and a quill pen. Ann wondered how many hands had clutched at that very quill before her, writing about the same brig and the same journey she was taking. Near the desk, a wooden chair with a cushioned seat provided a comfortable spot for Ann to sit down. The room was ventilated, which surprised Ann, who had already begun feeling a bit seasick. The room was quaint and simple but quite clean and neat.

There were some holes in the walls and floors. The floorboards creaked when she walked across them, and she was certain that she could hear a mouse scurrying around behind the walls. But Ann wasn't annoyed by its presence. After packing away her luggage, she went over to Mr. and Mrs. Raymond's room. Theirs was double her room's size and provided twice the amount of storage, windows, and desks, but other than that, it was laid out in a similar fashion. Their walls were painted in a light blue, whereas hers were unpainted. Their children's adjoined room was cramped. Their beds had been positioned against the walls to create as much space for them as possible. This would be their home for the next several weeks. Each night as children were put to bed, both their mother and Ann would pray over them, asking God to protect and give them a restful night's sleep.

Later on in the evening, Ann ventured back up on deck. The brig had picked up some more passengers along the way who were going to join the mission as well. Ann and the Raymonds met and spoke with them, exchanging stories of their past and hope for the future.

They spoke extensively about what would happen and what the plan entailed once they reached their destination. There were volunteers from all across America on board. A few even came from the southern states where slavery was still supported and sometimes practiced in secret. It was surprising how well these people got along with the rest of the missionaries on board. It only showed how God's love could overcome prejudices and lead His people, as it states in Micah 6:8, *"to act justly and to love mercy and to walk humbly with your God."* The Amistad men were also aboard the Frances Lord, their cabins close to those of the Raymonds.

The men were comfortable with the rest of the people onboard, having learned English thanks to Mr. Tappan and the people he recruited to teach them. The men spoke to the people around them, telling them of their home country, of the Mende people, and what the Americans could expect to see there. They kept their stories and information cheery and happy for now so as not to scare the missionaries departing from their home country for the first time.

The Amistad men were the most rowdy and joyous of the bunch, singing and dancing aboard the brig as they rejoiced that the Lord was enabling them to return to their country. Mr. Raymond got along with them superbly, and soon, Ann and Mrs. Raymond also became close to them. Ann befriended a man who introduced himself as George, and soon, the two were sharing detailed stories about their childhoods and home. Ann told him much about her religious faith and what she had learned and taught over the years in Church. They all ate together and prayed together, hoping that Jesus would be their morning start, guiding them through the darkness of the night in the vastness of the ocean and in the perils of the world they were about to encounter. So far, their prayers were heard as the weather remained pleasant and the water remained calm.

Over the next few weeks, Ann helped Mrs. Raymond a great deal. She helped her take care of the children and helped them study the Bible. They grew even closer to Ann as the vessel sailed across the Atlantic. Mr. Raymond spent the early mornings in God's Word studying and memorizing scriptures. He understood that the path laid before Him by God would be one fraught with danger and temptations. This particular morning, he turned to one of his favorite passages;

"I beseech you therefore, brethren, by the mercies of God, that ye present your bodies a living sacrifice, holy, acceptable unto God, which is your reasonable service. 2 And be not conformed to this world: but be ye transformed by the renewing of your mind, that ye may prove what is that good, and acceptable, and perfect, will of God."

– Romans 12:1-2

He had set his sights on the work ahead and knew he needed to be prepared. Only through the power of the Holy

Spirit within him could he accomplish the task set before him by God. After breakfast with the crew, he would speak with the captain about their progress. To this point, the weather had been rather delightful, with little threat of storms. The ship had responded well to the commands of the captain and crew. Mr. Raymond took the time each day to meet with the freed Amistad people to learn the Mende language and get a better understanding of their culture.

He would also lead them in lessons and spiritual exercises. In the evenings, the Raymonds would put their children to bed, say their prayers with them, and then ready themselves for the night. They would join in prayer, praising God for the ways He had protected and provided for them.

It would be many days before the brig would dock at a port as the cabin and crew went to replenish their supplies and perform repairs. It would also trade supplies that were being carried onboard.

The people aboard the Frances Lord would all rush to the deck when this happened, eager to get a glimpse of what life outside the United States looked like. Their eagerness was, of course, not unfounded as many of the ports were exceptionally beautiful, lined with stalls manned by various merchants from around the world.

Ann was having a wonderful time, and every day, she thanked God for giving her this marvelous opportunity and trusting her with the spread of His Holy Word. Though Ann was filled with awe, there was one thing that was causing her much pain. She had already begun to miss her mother and her home. She knew that it would be at least four to five weeks before she would be able to write to her or hear from her again, and she hoped and prayed that her mother was doing well back at home. While she worried aboard the Frances Lord, Mr. Tappan had already given Mrs. Harnden all the details about the sailing vessel and its journey so far. He assured her of the experience of the captain and crew and told her of the calm seas and pleasant weather.

Back in Massachusetts, Mrs. Harnden's heart ached as she knelt beside her bed every night and prayed for a safe journey for her daughter.

Chapter 3: God with Us

The first incident on the journey came to test the resilience and faith of those onboard. One morning, a man working to clean the masts on the brig stumbled, lost his balance, and fell into the swirling depths of the ocean.

Since it was so early in the morning, slightly before daybreak, there were only but a couple of other men on the deck tending to the duties. They heard the eerie splash as the man fell overboard, but due to the dim light and lack of helping hands, they could not see him in the waters.

They attempted to call out to him. They searched the deck and found some materials they knew would float and threw them overboard, hoping they would offer the man something to cling to.

Their efforts seemed to be in vain, as they could see no sign of the man. They sounded the bells and woke the captain and crew. Together, they valiantly made efforts to locate and save the man for the entirety of the morning, but they proved unsuccessful in their efforts.

The rest of the people onboard woke up due to the commotion and went onto the deck. Ann was filled with confusion as she listened from her room to the yells and shouts of the men on deck. She was frightened and thought for a long time that the brig had been boarded by pirates looking to sack the vessel and capture its passengers. She knelt in reverence for the Lord and prayed that her friends and fellow passengers might remain safe and that the pirates would be defeated.

Then, she listened more clearly and heard them sounding the bells that indicated that someone had fallen overboard. Her heart fell into the pit of her stomach, and she rushed out toward the chambers of Mr. and Mrs. Raymond. She knocked at the doors, asking them in a worried tone what was happening. Once they emerged, Mrs. Raymond hugged Ann and told her that all would be well and that God was with them. Together, they ventured out onto the deck to assess the situation and help in any way they could. Upon reaching there, they discovered that all the efforts to locate the man were unsuccessful even though they tried to help the crew. The sea was not raging, but the swell was high, and waves lashed against the vessel harshly. The sky, too, was grey, covered by clouds that blocked the sunlight. They decided to anchor the ship there and stay within the location in case the man reemerged. They had already thrown all sorts of floating objects into the ocean in the hopes that the man could hold onto them as he awaited rescue.

They gathered together in prayer for the man. The somber mood weighed heavily upon them as they joined hands, interlacing their fingers in unity. It was Mr. William Raymond, who took the lead in this solemn assembly, his unwavering faith and strong conviction helping the others find a sense of calm.

"Oh, Heavenly Father, we come before Thee in this hour of trial and tribulation, humbly seeking Thy guidance and strength," Mr. Raymond said in a powerful yet kind voice. *"We implore Thee to reach out a forgiving hand to our beloved brother, who has fallen into the deep dark seas. May he be enveloped by Thy heavenly protection and find reassurance in Thy embrace within the merciless waters."*

A chorus of "Amen" and murmurs of agreement echoed around the circle, the words resonating with profound sincerity. Each heart brimmed with hope, even in the face of despair, for their faith was the anchor that steadied their souls. Ann felt highly comforted, knowing that since the group all had such deep and profound devotion, the Lord would surely hear their prayers.

She added tearfully, *"Lord, we pray not only for our dear brother but also for his family and loved ones back home. Provide them with comfort and courage during this trying time. Let them know that we, your humble servants, unite in supplication on their behalf."* Ann was thinking of her own mother and the amount of worry and grief she would face if Ann had been lost at sea. The gentle rhythm of the brig swayed beneath their feet, akin to the rhythm of their prayers, finding solace in this shared connection with the Almighty. Their voices rose and fell like the tide, embracing both grief and hope.

Mr. and Mrs. Raymond, clasping hands, beseeched in unison, *"Grant us, O Lord, the strength to endure and the wisdom to comprehend Thy divine plan. Though we walk through the valley of the shadow of death, we shall fear no evil, for Thou art with us."*

This reminder filled the people with faith and comfort as they truly and deeply knew that the Lord would always be with them and that He would bless them with the safe return of the man whose name they now knew was Gerald. The prayers continued, fervently seeking divine intervention and the safe return of their lost companion. The missionaries offered supplications for the crew, the brig, and all souls onboard so that they might find solace and protection in God's hands.

The missionaries and crew stayed steady, certain that their prayers would be heard in Heaven. As the sun rose into the huge expanse of grey clouds, they were united in the belief that God's providence would prevail and lead them through this tough road, and they found comfort in their shared dedication. Together, they found solace in their collective devotion. As the sun climbed up into the sky and the hour approached noon, the crew and passengers separated into groups, trying to go about their day, but their minds were still consumed with thoughts of Gerald. Ann was in her room reading some of the scriptures that were her favorite, and that had always given her hope and courage. One of them most touched her heart in that moment:

> *⁷ "Be strong and very courageous. Be careful to obey all the law my servant Moses gave you; do not turn from it to the right or to the left, that you may be successful wherever you go. Keep this Book of the Law always on your lips; meditate on it day and night, so that you may be careful to do everything written in it. Then you will be prosperous and successful. Have I not commanded you? Be strong and courageous. Do not be afraid; do not be discouraged, for the LORD your God will be with you wherever you go."*
>
> **– Jousha 1:7-9**

Not only did the scripture make Ann think that God would help them save the man, but it also comforted her and helped her know for certain that the Lord would be with the entire crew and its passengers for the entire journey. The fact that the Word of God always gave Ann such solace was one of the reasons why she wanted to spread it as much as possible. At noon, as the relentless sun reached its zenith, casting its radiant glow upon the sea, a glimmer of hope emerged on the horizon. The crew, determined to locate their lost comrade, still scanned the vast expanse of water with unwavering determination.

Suddenly, amidst the undulating waves, a keen-eyed sailor spotted a faint object bobbing in the distance. Heartbeats quickened, and anticipation filled the air. The crew strained their eyes, yearning for confirmation of their discovery. As the ship drew nearer, the faint object revealed itself to be a man, clinging tenaciously to a wooden board that had been thrown into the waters earlier by one of the crew.

"Gerald! It's Gerald!" exclaimed one of the crewmen, his voice quivering with emotion. The missionaries and crew gathered at the ship's rail, their eyes brimming with relief and gratitude. The sight of their lost companion alive bolstered their spirits and reaffirmed their unwavering faith. The women, too, came out of their chambers to witness the scene. Some of them went immediately and fetched towels, blankets, water, and food.

With great precision and care, the crew launched a rescue mission. Ropes were tossed with expert aim, and hands reached out eagerly to draw Gerald back to the safety of the ship. Exhausted and drenched, he grasped the lifeline offered by his crew, his fingers gripping the wooden board that had been his salvation amidst the unforgiving depths.

"Thank the Lord!" Mr. Raymond exclaimed; his voice choked with emotion, saying, "God has answered our prayers and spared our dear brother."

As Gerald was hoisted aboard, the crew enveloped him in a warm embrace, their jubilation mingled with tears of gratitude. A few couldn't contain their emotions and wrapped their arms around Gerald, whispering prayers of thanksgiving and rejoicing in his miraculous survival. Once safely on deck, Gerald recounted his harrowing ordeal.

"When I fell overboard, I clung desperately to the wooden board the crew had thrown in for me. The waves were merciless, and I fought to stay afloat. But in my darkest moments, I felt a presence, a divine hand guiding me through the tumultuous waters."

"He was with you, Gerald, every step of the way," said Mrs. Raymond, her eyes shining with faith. "God's protection was upon you, and your faith kept you afloat."

Gerald nodded, his heart overflowing with gratitude. "Indeed, it was God's grace that sustained me. I felt His strength carrying me through the darkest of waters." In the aftermath of Gerald's rescue, the missionaries and crew gathered once more for a prayer of thanksgiving. Their voices rose in unison, offering praise to the Almighty for the safe return of their companion. They thanked God for the faith that bound them together and the power of prayer that brought them through adversity.

As the sun began its descent, painting the sky in hues of orange and gold, a newfound sense of unity and purpose filled the brig. They had weathered a storm of both sea and soul and through their unwavering faith, they had emerged stronger.

From that day forth, the bond between the missionaries and crew grew even stronger, cemented by the shared experience of divine providence. They continued their journey, guided by faith and a profound understanding that in the face of life's storms, their faith would serve as an unwavering compass, leading them safely toward their noble mission.

The whole incident had strengthened Ann's determination and devotion to God, and she was filled with more courage than she already possessed. She began reciting Joshua 1:7-9 every night before she retired to sleep. A few days later, another trial befell the crew and passengers of the Frances Lord. Ann awoke one morning bright and early. She proceeded to wash herself and pray. Then, as she was getting dressed, she noticed a piece of paper lying on the wooden floorboards of her dim cabin. Someone had slipped the note under her door. She was filled with confusion at the note, but she assumed that one of the Raymond children had slid it to her at night. Perhaps it was a little drawing or a letter to her from them. However, when she opened the folded piece of paper, it was not at all what she had expected. The contents shocked Ann to her core.

The note was highly inappropriate and improper. A crewman had sent it, telling Ann that she was highly beautiful and that he had eyes for her. The details will not be repeated, but the note left Ann feeling extremely insecure and violated. She began crying and feeling paranoid that she was being watched by some man with improper intentions. She decided to go to Mrs. Raymond to seek some comfort and advice. She knew that Mr. Raymond was above deck, leading the crew as they practiced some discipline-building exercises. Knocking at the door to their cabin, she was filled with embarrassment, but her tears were heavy, and her chest was constricted. She needed someone to be with her, and who better than Mrs. Raymond?

Upon hearing her light incessant knocks and opening the door, Mrs. Raymond's face fell. She beckoned Ann inside and listened to the young woman as she recounted what had happened and showed her the note. Mrs. Raymond comforted Ann and hugged the young woman as she sobbed, telling her that God would surely keep her safe. She convinced Ann to tell Mr. Raymond and the Captain of the Frances Lord about the message so that they could find the person who sent it and deliver justice. They would also be able to provide provisions to make Ann feel safer.

Gathering her courage, Ann decided to confide in Mr. Raymond and the Captain about the unsettling note. Together, they would seek justice and ensure the safety of all women aboard the Frances Lord. Wiping her tears away, Ann made her way to the deck where Mr. Raymond and the Captain, stern yet compassionate leaders, were engaged in studying their spiritual disciplines. With a deep breath, Ann approached Mr. Raymond and respectfully sought his attention. "Brother William," she began, "I have something troubling to share."

Mr. Raymond noticed the distress in her eyes and took her aside, away from the prying eyes of the crew. "What is it, dear sister?" he inquired gently.

Ann handed him the offensive note, and his expression darkened as he read its contents. "This is unacceptable," he said firmly, his eyes revealing a deep sense of responsibility to protect the flock under his care. Captain Brown, observing the unfolding conversation, joined them, his weathered face showing concern. "What seems to be the matter?" he asked, his tone firm but caring. Ann recounted the distressing incident, and Captain Brown's jaw tensed. "Such behavior will not be tolerated on my ship," he stated resolutely. "We shall find the man responsible and address this matter with utmost seriousness."

Both Mr. Raymond and the Captain shared a common understanding of the responsibility bestowed upon them as leaders, not only to ensure the safe passage of their voyage but also to protect the spiritual well-being and dignity of those onboard.

Determined to uncover the truth, they assembled the crew and questioned each member individually, their stern inquiries backed by a profound sense of justice and integrity. As the crew realized the gravity of the situation, their unity strengthened, knowing that they were bound by principles that transcended mere maritime protocols.

With a keen eye for detail and a compassionate heart, Mr. Raymond and the Captain narrowed down the possible perpetrators. They reminded the crew that they were all brothers on this voyage, guided by the light of God's teachings. Finally, the truth emerged, and the man who had penned the inappropriate note was identified. It was the 2nd mate who had sent the note. Confronted with the evidence and the disappointment of his crew, he expressed genuine remorse for his actions. In a display of true Christian forgiveness, Mr. Raymond and the Captain, firm in their admonishment, offered the man an opportunity for redemption, urging him to amend his ways and seek forgiveness from God and Ann. The crew, witnessing this display of grace, found strength in the example set by their leaders. There was a newfound sense of respect and camaraderie enveloping the Frances Lord. The incident served as a reminder of the importance of God's teachings in guiding their voyage and forging the bonds of unity and compassion among them.

As the sun dipped below the horizon, casting a warm glow upon the deck, Ann felt a sense of relief. She had found solace in her faith and the unwavering support of her fellow missionaries, as well as the stern yet compassionate leadership of Mr. Raymond and the Captain. With their eyes fixed on the distant horizon, the crew of the Frances Lord pressed on, guided by the light of God, ready to face whatever trials and tribulations lay ahead, knowing that their faith would carry them through. That night, Ann felt a sense of comfort, but she also began missing her mother and her warm embrace that would have made the whole incident even easier.

She began writing a letter to her mother that she would send at the next dock. The letter turned out to be extremely long as Ann poured her heart out due to her heightened emotions. Part of it said,

> *"I have often thought how I should like to have you look in upon us and see how comfortable we are. We have a pleasant vessel – a pleasant captain and pleasant weather. Mr. and Mrs. Raymond are very kind to me – they could not be kinder if I were their own child. But what is better than all the rest our heavenly Father is with us bearing us onward toward the port of our destination. When I realize that it my own dear mother that I am addressing I am a wonder to myself that I can write to you not knowing as I ever shall see you again on earth and not be almost overwhelmed in tears. I know I could not without the help of God. Oh! What a blessed we have got. How true it is that He will enable us to perform all that He requires of us to do."*

Ann's Lost letter to her mother, written aboard the brig Frances Lord. Dated November 1843

Ann had been filled with the grace of God, but her and the cabin's troubles were not yet complete. The 2nd mate's shame and guilt turned to bitterness, and he sought solace in spreading malicious rumors about Mr. Raymond, the pious and dedicated leader of the missionaries. Unfounded whispers of nightly visits to Ann's room tainted the air, but the crew and fellow missionaries stood steadfast in their trust and respect for Mr. Raymond.

The Wesleyan Missionaries, a devout and resolute group of believers, were with the people and had joined the Mende Mission. Their own mission was to spread the Gospel to distant lands, guided by the principles of unwavering faith, compassion, and forgiveness. As rumors swirled like tempestuous winds, the missionaries found strength in their shared commitment to God's teachings and the truth that lay therein.

They rallied around Mr. Raymond, offering him unwavering support and encouragement. With hearts bound by a common belief, they reminded one another of their duty to dispel falsehoods and uphold the virtues of their faith. They fervently prayed for the truth to prevail and for the hearts of those who had strayed from righteousness to be guided back onto the righteous path. Through the darkest days, Mr. Raymond maintained his composure, drawing strength from the faith that had led him to this noble mission. He held fast to the belief that God's light would eventually dispel the shadows of slander that threatened to engulf him.

Meanwhile, Captain Brown observed the turbulent seas of gossip and deceit. He could see the inner turmoil tormenting the 2nd mate and recognized that it was a reflection of the man's own failings and remorse. He sternly reprimanded the man for spreading false gossip and warned him of the grim consequences of bearing false witness against a fellow brother in Christ. The crew and the missionaries helped bring the truth to light. Witnesses spoke forward about Mr. Raymond's unshakable commitment to his duties and the deep religious values that would never see him be unfaithful to his wife or misbehave with any woman, let alone one he had personally encouraged to join the mission. The rumors crumbled under the weight of truth, and the crew could no longer deny the integrity and piety of their respected leader. It was at this moment that grace and forgiveness came into play. Rather than seeking vengeance, Mr. Raymond and the Captain chose to extend kindness and mercy to the 2nd mate.

They recognized that the man's actions were driven by shame and regret. Therefore, rather than casting him away, they told him to embrace his faith more fervently. They encouraged him to seek redemption through the teachings of God. They understood that, in the vast ocean of human frailty, the waves of compassion and forgiveness could heal even the deepest wounds. As the days passed, harmony and tranquility once again graced the Frances Lord. The crew and the missionaries worked side by side, bound by their shared faith and commitment to their divine calling. Through the challenges faced and the storms weathered, the voyage of the Frances Lord continued, with each passing day strengthening the resolve of the missionaries. The trials they encountered only served to deepen their faith and dedication to the principles they held dear. United by their mission, faith, and the grace that had brought them through turbulent waters, they set their course forward, ready to embrace whatever lay ahead. With their unwavering commitment to God's teachings and the virtues of compassion and forgiveness, they sailed onward, knowing that their journey would continue to be guided by the divine light that shone within each and every one of them. After the incident, Ann was once again filled with emotion and continued her letter to her mother. She wrote:

"I have often thought if God has chosen some other one more capable than myself it seems as though they might do something – in the sphere to which I have been called. It seems to me I can do nothing at all and I cannot of myself but this had been a most blessed passage to me, "through Christ strengthening me I can do all things." I can go forward in the strength of this promise feeling I can daily ask for that wisdom which comes from God who giveth all men liberally. Knowing that whatsoever I ask in faith I shall receive."

Ann's lost letter to her mother, written aboard the brig Frances Lord. Dated November 1843

After being tested to this extent, Ann knew that the Lord, Jesus Christ was truly beside her at all times. She felt fulfilled in the Holy Spirit, and this propelled her forward to continue with her mission, having no doubt in her mind that it would all go well.

The crew became even more tightly knit after these unfortunate instances, and their energy became even higher than what it was before.

The weekly Sunday sermons and daily morning prayers became even more passionate and devout. Those on the crew who were not as deeply invested in the mission as the others also seemed far more connected when they prayed and praised the lord. They discussed how the devil had been active on the brig Frances Lord, trying to derail the journey and make those onboard lose hope and faith in God. They all rejoiced in the fact that they had passed the tests that had been laid out before them. They had truly overcome them through the courage and grace that God had gifted to them, and in the process, they had forsaken the Devil and his nefarious ways. After this, the journey they were on had no more mishaps or difficulties.

God has even blessed the weather, and as a result, the brig faced no storms, hail, or gales as it journeyed further into the Atlantic Ocean. The reliance of the crew touched Ann. She truly felt like she was one of them and that they were there for her to aid her through any trials and troubles that she may have. She was eternally grateful for that, and for the beautiful family, she had found in the Raymonds. In the reliance and determination of the crew, we see the shining light of the Lord, and we see his mercy. They served as an example of what people could achieve if they only gave their whole heart to the Lord and trusted Him to guide them through all. They surrendered to God instead of trying to control their own circumstances, and this enabled them to find safe passage. A passage so safe that it was, in fact, almost unheard of, which was proof that the Lord was with them as they sailed across the Atlantic Ocean.

Chapter 4: The Embrace

While embarking on her own transformative journey to Mende, Africa, the story of the Israelites' exodus from Egypt and their crossing of the Jordan River resonated deeply within Ann's heart.

The parallel between her voyage and their journey through the desert served as a poignant reminder of the profound impact that faith and trust in God could have on one's path.

As she navigated the challenges of her missionary work, Ann pondered the pivotal moment when the Israelites stood at the banks of the Jordan River for the first time.

Their hesitancy to cross, driven by fear and doubt, mirrored the internal struggles she herself faced.

"[31] But the men who had gone up with him said, 'We can't attack those people; they are stronger than we are.' [32] And they spread among the Israelites a bad report about the land they had explored. They said, 'The land we explored devours those living in it. All the people we saw there are of great size. [33] We saw the Nephilim there (the descendants of Anak come from the Nephilim). We seemed like grasshoppers in our own eyes, and we looked the same to them.'"

– Numbers 13:31–33

Like them, Ann also felt that she was weak and that she did not have the strength to endure her life-altering journey at times. Just as they had grappled with the decision to trust in God's guidance, Ann had questioned her ability to fully surrender to His plan. The scouts' cautionary words echoed in Ann's thoughts, a stark reminder of the doubts that could undermine her resolve.

Yet, the Israelites' misstep also taught her the importance of unyielding faith and the consequences of allowing fear to govern her choices. Ann found herself at a crossroads, much like the Israelites, torn between the voice of doubt and the call to trust. At the first encounter of the Jordan, the Israelites failed to trust in God, gave into the fear, and ended up wandering in the desert for 40 years. Even in their mistrust of God, He did not abandon them. He was with them throughout those 40 years, providing for their needs. Here in the desert, He guided them, shaped them, and loved them. When the time came, He brought them back to the same place they had once given in to fear. Once again, they were called to trust Him and enter the Promised Land.

Ann read the verses that showed the love and protection of God during this journey to the promised land again and again.

"14So the people left their camp to cross the Jordan, and the priests who were carrying the Ark of the Covenant went ahead of them. 15It was the harvest season, and the Jordan

was overflowing its banks. But as soon as the feet of the priests who were carrying the Ark touched the water at the river's edge, ^{16}the water above that point began backing up a great distance away at a town called Adam, which is near Zarethan. And the water below that point flowed on to the Dead Sea until the riverbed was dry. Then all the people crossed over near the town of Jericho.

"^{17}Meanwhile, the priests who were carrying the Ark of the Lord's Covenant stood on dry ground in the middle of the riverbed as the people passed by. They waited there until the whole nation of Israel had crossed the Jordan on dry ground."

– Joshua 2: 14-17

The words filled her with a sense of ease and reminded her that if one follows the path that God has set out for them, He will be with them during every step of the journey.

In her moments of reflection, Ann saw the Israelites' subsequent return to the Jordan as a powerful lesson in redemption and resilience. Their renewed commitment to keep their eyes fixed on God and His covenant reminded her that setbacks and doubt need not define her journey. The Israelites' triumph over the river became a testament to God's strength and His ability to guide them through tumultuous waters. As Ann drew parallels between her struggles and the Israelites' experiences, she understood that her faith, like theirs, was a bridge between the challenges she faced and the divine promises that lay ahead. Just as the Israelites had to fix their gaze on God and the covenant, Ann realized the importance of anchoring her journey in unwavering trust. The symbolism of the Jordan River held a special place in Ann's heart. She could sense the call to embrace her own Jordan moments—the obstacles and uncertainties that loomed before her—as opportunities for growth and transformation. The story of the Israelites served as a beacon of hope, reminding her that her faith could part the waters of doubt and lead her to victory.

With each passing day, Ann resolved to mirror the Israelites' courage and resilience. She found solace in knowing that God's promises were not confined to the pages of history but were alive and applicable to her journey. Just as they had stepped into the river with faith as their guide, Ann, too, chose to step forward with unwavering trust in God's divine plan, regardless of the challenges that lay ahead.

In her moments of uncertainty, Ann's reflections on the Israelites' journey became a source of strength and inspiration. Their story served as a reminder that the path to triumph began with a resolute faith that could overcome even the most daunting obstacles. Just as the Israelites had crossed the Jordan, Ann embraced the journey with the certainty that God's guidance would lead her to victory.

Two weeks had passed since the ship set sail, and in that span of time, Ann had traversed a landscape of challenges and triumphs, mirroring the struggles and victories of those who had gone before her.

As she looked back, Ann's heart swelled with gratitude for the progress they had made. Their voyage had been punctuated by moments that tested their faith, yet her unwavering trust in God remained steadfast. One such incident had unfolded when a man had fallen overboard.

The potential for disaster had loomed large, but the crew's collective prayers acted as a lifeline, leading to the man's safe rescue. Ann's heart was a canvas of thanksgiving; she recognized the power of unity and the strength that faith could bring even in the face of dire circumstances. Even when she had found the inappropriate note, fear could have gripped her heart, but her faith prevailed. The captain's intervention, coupled with the man's subsequent repentance, became a testament to the resolution of the incident. Ann's unwavering reliance on God's guidance transformed obstacles into opportunities for growth. Ann's journey was an embodiment of her response to God's call, despite the hurdles that arose. Her thoughts meandered through the landscape of her experiences, and she often thought back to the biggest hurdle she had already overcome, such as leaving behind her family and friends. Even in the vastness of the sea, the yearning for her mother's presence remained an undercurrent, tugging at her heartstrings. Yet, her resolve remained unyielding; much like the Israelites' journey through the desert, she recognized that her own journey required sacrifices. She was eternally grateful to Mr. Raymond and how he had supported her through the journey and through every struggle that she faced.

Just as he had promised her mother, he had treated her with the utmost care, becoming a fatherly figure guiding her through uncharted waters. The assurance of his protective presence eased her heart, reminding her that she was not alone on this expedition of faith.

Mrs. Raymond, the children, and the other missionaries had also welcomed Ann with open arms and made her feel like a part of a new family of God united in their love and trust in Him. By fostering profound connections with them, her faith had grown and flourished even deeper. The journey was not without its struggles, yet Ann's trust in God continued to flourish. As the ship sailed forward, Ann's heart remained anchored in her trust in God. Just as the Israelites believed that their faith could part the waters, she, too, believed that her faith would carry her through the challenges she encountered.

When she questioned herself, Ann's heart found refuge in gratitude. Her journey was not just a physical voyage but a journey of the spirit—a journey marked by gratitude for every trial, every victory, and every lesson learned. Ann's heart remained an altar of thanksgiving, a testament to the transformative power of faith and the profound blessings that came with answering God's call. As the night settled over the ship, Ann retreated to her cabin, seeking solace in the warm embrace of solitude.

The dim glow of a lantern cast flickering shadows upon the pages of her Bible, a cherished companion on her journey. The silence of the night was punctuated by the gentle sway of the ship, a rhythmic reminder of the voyage's continuous progression.

In the hushed solitude of her cabin, Ann delved into the words of Matthew's Gospel. The verses illuminated before her eyes seemed to echo the thoughts that had taken root in her heart. She read:

"16 So the last shall be first, and the first last: for many be called, but few chosen."

– Matthew 20:16

This resonated deeply, revealing a profound truth about the nature of God's calling and how Ann had indeed been one of the chosen few whom God had trusted to spread His Holy Word to the ends of the earth. Ann's journey had been one of relinquishing the familiar for the beckoning unknown. The concept that God's call might lead one to forsake family, relinquish comfort zones, and embark on a journey of faith wasn't lost on her. The echoes of her own story intertwined with the scriptural narrative, harmonizing in a symphony of purpose and sacrifice.

"And everyone who has left houses or brothers or sisters or father or mother or wife or children or fields for my sake will receive a hundred times as much and will inherit eternal life."

– Matthew 19:29

These words became a beacon of insight for Ann. In those quiet moments, as the ship gently rocked beneath her, she contemplated the gravity of the verse.

Her heart carried the weight of her decision to follow God's call. Ann pondered the depth of her willingness to leave behind her mother and the comfort of her familiar life, choosing instead to heed God's beckoning. Her life had been one of comfort, sheltered by the embrace of family, friends, and a loving, Godly community. The seed of faith had taken root within her, propelling her to embrace the uncharted path that lay before her. As Ann continued to read and reflect, the words of the verse resonated as both a challenge and a promise. The sacrifice she had made was not without its cost, yet her heart was steadfast in the belief that the rewards of obedience far outweighed the temporary losses.

The notion of receiving a hundredfold in return for her willingness to forsake comfort was a promise that sustained her during moments of doubt and uncertainty. In the stillness of her cabin, Ann's spirit soared. The verses she read that night encapsulated the essence of her journey—a journey that mirrored the Israelites' voyage, marked by trials, sacrifice, and an unwavering trust in God's guidance. The path she had chosen, though laden with challenges and separations, was also a testament to the fulfillment that comes from answering God's call.

With the moonlight streaming through the cabin window, Ann closed her Bible and offered a silent prayer. Her heart was buoyed by the assurance that every sacrifice, every step taken in faith, was not in vain. The stillness of the night carried with it the promise of hundredfold blessings and eternal life, a promise that resonated within her soul and fueled her journey of faith. While she was resolute in her faith and purpose, the ties of the family remained unbreakable. The notion of leaving the family for the sake of God's call still weighed heavily on her heart. Despite the importance of her call, Ann couldn't help but think of the loved ones she had left behind.

Ann's heart found solace in knowing that, despite the distance, the bonds of the family remained strong. The verses' meaning grew richer as she pondered the complexities of obedience and the enduring ties that family held. In the quiet of her cabin, Ann's prayers embraced both her journey of faith and the family she cherished deeply.

As her fingers traced the words of the passage, Ann's thoughts turned to her mother and her siblings, especially her sister, Mary. She wondered how they were now that she had left, and she wondered how things had changed for them. She wrote a letter to her mother and said:

I sometimes think that perhaps you will think I have lost all love for you but it is not so. The more I think of you the more I love you and the more I love my heavenly Father for having given me a Christian mother to train me up for the service for had you dear mother been an opposer to religion I should not have been where I am now unless God had as by miracle snatched me as a brand from the burning. It was impressions I received from you in my childhood that first led me to look at myself as a lost sinner and to pray to God for forgiveness.

How often dear mother you told me to be a good girl and to pray to God to make me good. That word good girl went to my heart I would often think of the advice of my dear mother and think commandment "children obey your parents in all things" would come home to me. I felt I was continually disobeying you; not only you but God for I knew I could not be good so long as I was in rebellion against God and I could not bear to think of disobeying that mother I loved so well. I knew I loved you and wanted to obey you so I prayed to God to forgive me and after a long struggle with unbelief I was led to trust in Christ and found peace in believing.

You may think it strong that I should write this now but I do it to encourage to continue to be faithful to the cause of

Christ and to your remaining children and because my attention has been called to the importance of persevering in prayer and in our labors to save souls.

When you feel your heart drawn out by the Spirit of God to pray for a soul, I believe you are bound to persevere in prayer and exercise faith that God will save that soul. You may know that you are led by the Spirit if your heart is drawn out in love for that soul and in love to God accompanied by a melting down of the soul. Now dear mother when you begin to think you can do nothing think of that one word that God used to put me upon thinking about my soul. I believe I have learnt some new lessons about these things myself and this is the reason why I write them to you.

I don't know but you have already learnt them. If you have you will be glad to know that I have. I wish them also that you may be encouraged to pray for Mary. I believe she will yet be a child of God and the other children. I must say here that I have felt very differently from what I ever did before about Mary. I believe she will yet be a child of God. I believe it will be for the glory of God to save her but I know He will not save her contrary to her own will. I believe she will yet see the error of her ways and turn to God and live. I know that Christ's blood is sufficient to cleanse from all sin.

- Extract from a letter from Miss Ann Harnden to her mother dated November 1843

In the stillness of her cabin, Ann's thoughts were on her sister Mary, a soul entangled in the complexities of life. As Ann meditated on her faith journey, she couldn't help but reflect on Mary's path as well. The words of Matthew's Gospel had resonated, sparking a belief deep within her heart. Despite the challenges and the distance that separated them, Ann held fast to the conviction that Mary's heart could be transformed if she would only open it up to the grace God offered her. Ann believed in the transformative potential of faith, recognizing that even the farthest hearts could be drawn close to God's embrace. The verse's message echoed through her mind, carrying with it the promise of redemption and renewal. Ann envisioned a future where Mary's life could be illuminated by the same divine light that guided her own steps. In her prayers, Ann whispered the hope that her sister, once far from God's grace, could find a path that led her to become a child of God.

As the ship gently swayed in the moonlit night, Ann's faith intertwined with her love for Mary. The verse's significance went beyond mere words; it was a beacon of hope, a reminder that transformation was possible even in the most challenging of circumstances. Her heart held onto the belief that God's love had the power to mend, restore, and awaken souls, no matter how distant they may have strayed. In the depths of her contemplation, Ann's prayers extended beyond herself and her journey. They reached out to Mary, her sister, who remained close in spirit despite the physical distance. In her prayers was an earnest plea for her sister to find solace, love, and redemption within the embrace of God's unwavering grace. She also envisioned her mother's unwavering love and strength becoming an anchor for Mary's troubled heart. Ann's heart ached with the understanding that her mother's love could be a beacon of light for Mary, guiding her back from the path she had wandered. She longed for her mother to hold onto hope, to persistently reach out to Mary even in the face of adversity. That night, Ann's prayers extended beyond the confines of her cabin, soaring to the heavens as whispered petitions. She prayed that her mother would not give up on Mary and that the powerful bond of maternal love could penetrate even the deepest layers of hurt and estrangement.

Ann yearned for her mother to be a guiding force, a source of unyielding support and encouragement for Mary's journey toward reconciliation and redemption. She pleaded for her mother to remain steadfast and extend a hand of love and understanding toward Mary. She envisioned a future where Mary's heart could be mended, where the love of a mother and the grace of God could work together to rewrite her story.

Her heart remained tethered to her family, her prayers carrying a message of love, redemption, and the unyielding power of familial bonds. Ann found solace in the belief that the Holy Spirit was a guiding presence in the lives of her family, just as it was in her own journey. She knew that

God's spirit could lead even the wayward hearts back to the path of righteousness. Her prayers extended to her family, a fervent plea for the Holy Spirit to work in Mary's life, drawing her toward the love and grace that awaited her.

However, as Ann pondered the intricate dance of divine intervention, her thoughts shifted to the stark reality of human frailty. Just as the Holy Spirit could guide us toward goodness, the sinister force of temptation wielded by Satan could lead us astray. Her heart ached at the knowledge that Mary's journey could be laden with hurdles as the adversary sought to entice her away from the path of redemption.

She recognized that the journey toward transformation was not devoid of challenges; the lure of temptation often masked itself in alluring forms, aiming to derail the course of righteousness. It was a commitment to follow God's guidance through the maze of life's twists and turns, all the while combating the temptations that sought to veer one off the course that was the true essence of being a child of God. She was resolute that the devil had been at work on the ship and had attempted to steer her off her course to righteousness.

In her letter to her mother, she wrote:

You may ask what temptations has to do with my going to Africa. To answer you I want to say they have now much to do with me and I should think strong if the devil has not been harassing you about it. He has brought up everything before my mind that he could to try to make me to believe that God had not called me. But I have looked to God and He has delivered me out of all his temptations.

- Extract from a letter from Miss Ann Harnden to her mother dated November 1843

The next morning, the brig was to land in Gambia. This would be their first taste of the land they had journeyed so far to inhabit and teach in. As the brig sailed toward Gambia, a palpable sense of excitement permeated the air. The prospect of reaching their destination, the culmination of their journey, was a beacon of hope that lit up the hearts of both the crew and the mission members. The expansive sea stretched before them, its azure depths mirroring the anticipation that bubbled within.

On the deck, Mr. Raymond stood with a glimmer in his eyes, his weathered face bearing the weight of countless prayers and fervent aspirations. He shared a knowing smile with Ann, a silent acknowledgment of the challenges they had overcome and the promise that lay ahead. Mrs. Raymond, a steadfast pillar of support, stood beside him, her gaze fixed on the distant horizon.

Their children played nearby, their laughter harmonizing with the sound of the waves. As they sailed toward Gambia's shores, Mr. Raymond turned to Ann, his voice carrying the echoes of gratitude and determination. "Ann, my sister, can you feel it? We're nearing the land that holds the hopes of many. God has led us this far, and I believe He will guide us as we step onto that foreign soil." Ann's eyes shimmered with a mix of emotions—joy, anticipation, and a touch of trepidation. "Yes, Mr. Raymond," she replied with a fervent nod. "It's incredible to think how far we've come. The challenges, the doubts... all of it has led us here. I can't help but believe that this is where God wants us to be."

Mrs. Raymond interjected with a smile, her voice warm and reassuring. "And remember, Ann, even when the path seems uncertain, God's hand is never far away. He's been our constant companion, guiding us through stormy seas and calm waters alike."

Their children, caught up in the infectious excitement, tugged at Ann's sleeves. "Miss Ann, do you think we'll meet new friends in Gambia?" one of them asked, eyes wide with wonder.

Ann crouched down, her smile radiant. "Absolutely! Gambia is a new chapter in our journey, filled with opportunities to make new friends and share God's love." As the brig sailed on, the missionary's anticipation was palpable, their conversations a chorus of dreams and expectations. With its promise of purpose and challenges, the distant land of Gambia loomed larger with every passing wave. The sea seemed to conspire with their excitement, gently propelling them toward their destination.

In this moment, the crew and mission members were united in their shared purpose, their collective hope, and their unyielding faith. The horizon held the unknown but also the fulfillment of their calling, a journey that had forged unbreakable bonds and transformed hearts along the way. As the brig ventured closer to the Gambia River, a hushed sense of awe settled over the crew and mission members. The sight of the river's entrance, flanked by lush greenery and the promise of the unknown, stirred a mix of emotions.

As they navigated the river's meandering path, the scenery transformed into a breathtaking tableau of vibrant landscapes.

Dense foliage framed the waterway, their leaves rustling in harmony with the gentle lapping of the waves. The riverbanks seemed to stretch out in welcome, embracing the vessel as it made its way deeper inland. On the deck, Mr. Raymond stood with Ann by his side, both of them silently taking in the splendor around them.

The river's serene beauty was a testament to the Creator's handiwork, a reflection of the beauty within the hearts of the people they hoped to touch. Mr. Raymond turned to Ann, his voice echoed a reverent whisper, saying, "Ann, do you see the way the river flows? Just like our journey of faith, it may curve and twist, but it ultimately leads to our destination. And like the river's waters nourish the land, I believe our presence here will bring hope and nourishment to the souls of Gambia." Ann nodded, her gaze fixed on the passing scenery. As they journeyed deeper into the heart of Gambia, Mrs. Raymond joined them on deck, her eyes alight with wonder. "This land holds so much promise, doesn't it? I can't help but think of the lives we're meant to touch, the stories waiting to unfold."

As they ventured further, they remained united in their quest to share God's love and grace with open hearts and open arms. As the brig sailed upon the gentle waves of the river, they were being led to fulfill the call of God upon their lives no matter what lay ahead.

Chapter 5: Mission Begins

Mende unfurled before the missionaries; it was like a paradise created directly by the hands of the Almighty God. Its landscape was proof of the Creator's artistry—a lush and vibrant land bathed in the golden glow of the African sun. Tall, swaying palms greeted them as they disembarked from the ship, their leaves whispering tales of the ancient land's secrets.

The air was filled with the exotic scent of tropical blooms, their colors an explosion of life against the backdrop of emerald forests. Exotic birds adorned the trees, their melodic calls harmonizing with the rustling leaves. In this new land, every breeze carried the promise of revelation, every sunrise a promise of a new adventure guided by the Lord's hand.

Mende was a land of rolling hills and fertile plains, where rivers meandered through verdant valleys, offering sustenance to the land and its people. The soil beneath their feet teemed with life, and it was upon this sacred ground that the seeds of faith would be sown.

The missionaries, led by Mr. Raymond, approached the natives of Mende with hearts full of humility and a deep desire to share the Gospel. Their interactions were marked by respect for the local customs and traditions, recognizing that the path to the natives' hearts lay through understanding and the work of the Holy Spirit. Language became a bridge between the missionaries and the people of Mende. The free Amistad captives who came with the missionaries helped them and acted as translators for the missionaries so that they could interact with the people.

While on the ship, they had begun to teach some of the mission members the language of the natives, Sherbro. Ann, in particular, immersed herself in learning the Sherbro language on the ship and now with the natives. She often engaged with young children to grasp the nuances of communication and spoke with the women of the tribe to learn new words and to hear their stories. This effort endeared her to the community, as they witnessed her genuine commitment to understanding their way of life. Ann displayed that the missionaries' approach was not one of imposition but of loving your neighbor. They sought to work alongside the natives, learning from them as much as they shared the Gospel message of grace and love.

The bonds that formed were deeply rooted in the shared experiences of life, such as tending to the needs of children or sharing meals. Through those bonds, the message of the love of Christ, His grace, and the offer of salvation would be shared. The king who ruled a local tribe in Mende was a figure of great authority and respect. His presence commanded attention, and his regal bearing reflected the centuries-old traditions he upheld. His attire directly displayed his status. He was always adorned with intricately woven fabrics and embellishments that told the story of his lineage. He was a man of wisdom, entrusted with the well-being of his tribe and the stewardship of a vast estate. His voice carried the weight of tradition and the hopes of his people. He was known for his generosity, often hosting gatherings where the community would come together to celebrate life's blessings.

It was in these gatherings that Mr. Raymond and other missionaries took the opportunity to share about Jesus and His invitation to all people to come to Him and celebrate God's blessings.

The king's estate, nestled within the natural splendor of Mende, was a monument to his role as a caretaker of the land. The sprawling acres were meticulously tended, providing sustenance for the tribe and showcasing the fertility of the land.

His relationship with the missionaries was one of mutual respect, as they recognized the significance of his role in the community, and he treated them well since they came with a wealth of knowledge and a mindset that displayed their respect for the differing customs and traditions of the Mende people. The missionaries learned that the key element in Mende's religion was the belief in the existence of a supreme being, Ngewo. Although transcendent and outside the immediate reach of human beings, Ngewo established an order of spiritual beings and powers through which he interacted with the created order. At the heart of Mende's belief about Ngewo is that he is the creator and sustainer of all life. All life and activity, in both a material and non-material sense, derived from him. Ngewo created the world and everything in it, including not only human beings, animals, and plants but also spirits.

They were told that Ngewo is actively involved in the affairs of the world. Mende holds that although Ngewo is outside their immediate contact, on a day-to-day basis, he is believed to work through a variety of executors through whom power is dispensed to humanity.

This is a significant point as it helps unveil the relatedness of the belief systems. Because Ngewo is outside immediate human reach, but at the same time, he cares for his creation. He has provided certain powers and mediums through which he executes this care.

Another outstanding characteristic of Ngewo is his pursuit of truth. Thus, the notion of justice and its application in society is endowed with divine origin because it has its roots in Ngewo. The similarities between Ngewo and the God of the Bible led to many interesting discussions. The missionaries would use their beliefs to help explain who God is and how He works in the world.

Since the mission had brought with them the freed Amistad people, the tribe and the king were even more assured and convinced that these Westerners were not here to steal their people and ravage their lands as the colonizers and slave traders of the past did. You can understand their concern by knowing the history of the slave trade in their nation.

There were over 400,000 people kidnapped from Sierra Leone during the 1700s. They were enslaved and sent to other British colonies, the Caribbean, and North America. Entire families vanished overnight, while others were left without fathers or sons.[1] They welcomed their fellow brethren with open arms, and as the Amistad revealed their stories from their time in the terrible slave ship, the discriminatory American courts, and the kind mission grounds, the Mende people and the Tribesmen leaders and elders became warmer to the American Mission's people. The king was the warmest of them all.

The relationship between the missionaries and the tribal king was marked by diplomacy, respect, and a shared desire for the well-being of the community. The king, a guardian of tradition and culture, extended his hospitality to the missionaries upon their arrival, and after speaking to them, he began treating them extremely well.

Mr. Raymond, with his innate ability to bridge cultural gaps, engaged in heartfelt conversations with the king. They

---

[1] Cited from: https://www.amrevmuseum.org/sierra-leone-and-the%20americanrevolution#

exchanged stories of their respective backgrounds, finding common ground in their commitment to the welfare of their people. The king's estate became a place where ideas were shared and bonds of friendship were forged. Mr. Raymond understood what Paul meant when he stated:

> *"At the same time, pray also for us, that God may open to us a door for the word, to declare the mystery of Christ, on account of which I am in prison— that I may make it clear, which is how I ought to speak."*
>
> **– Col. 4:3-4**

As emissaries of the Christian faith, the missionaries approached their interactions with humility. They understood that their mission was not to replace the king's authority but to offer spiritual guidance and support. The king, in turn, appreciated their commitment to the community's spiritual growth and recognized the positive changes that their presence brought. A spirit of cooperation and mutual respect characterized interactions between the missionaries and the people of Mende.

The missionaries' approach was one of humility and a genuine desire to learn from the natives. They treated each other with kindness and empathy, recognizing the value of cultural exchange. The Christian call to be servants to all resonated across every aspect of the missionaries' lives. In their studies, they had read Christ's words in,

"But whoever would be great among you must be your servant, and whoever would be first among you must be your slave, even as the Son of Man came not to be served but to serve, and to give his life as a ransom for many."

– Matthew 20:26-28

The king's hospitality was met with gratitude, and the missionaries reciprocated by sharing their knowledge and faith. As a community, they celebrated life's blessings together.

The bonds that formed displayed the power of understanding and the potential for unity, even in the face of cultural differences. It showed that when one was confident in God's power and faithful that His blessings would fall upon those who followed the path He had destined for them, their journeys would be full of meaningful and positive findings and experiences. Most of the meetings with the king happened in what Ann referred to as his 'public house,' as this was the space where he hosted and celebrated. The king's public house, nestled within the heart of the tribal grounds, was a small yet grand structure that bore the weight of tradition and hospitality.

Crafted from locally sourced timber and adorned with intricate carvings, its architecture spoke volumes of the tribe's cultural heritage. The thatched roof, skillfully woven from palm fronds, sheltered the interior from the equatorial sun, casting dappled shadows across the courtyard.

The public house served as a place of great significance, playing host to leaders and kings from neighboring tribes and other important figures in the region. Its spacious interior featured a central hearth, where a fire perpetually burned, symbolizing the warmth of welcome extended to all who crossed its threshold.

The walls bore the marks of time, adorned with ancestral artifacts, vibrant woven tapestries, and intricately crafted statues and hangings depicting the tribe's rich history. Handcrafted wooden stools and benches, polished to a gleam, provided seating for dignitaries and guests during gatherings and meetings. Ornate masks and sculptures adorned the walls, bearing witness to the artistry and cultural significance of the tribe. Whenever important gatherings occurred, such as diplomatic meetings or celebrations of unity, the missionaries were welcomed into the king's public house. Within these walls, the exchange of ideas and spiritual dialogue took place as the missionaries and tribal leaders sought common ground in the pursuit of communal well-being. The space also served as an inspiration for the designs of the school and residence that they wished to build in Mende.

The missionaries envisioned a place of residence and education that would seamlessly blend with the breathtaking natural beauty of Mende. The mission spoke at length with the king about their plans and discussed with him the best ways in which they could build, the best materials to use that would make the place durable, and the best labor to hire to aid them in their tasks. Together, they drew up the plans and began with their work.

The king gave them a space on the land that would be the prime location for their headquarters. Located near the tranquil riverbanks, the site was chosen for its serene ambiance and scenic views. Towering trees, their branches forming a lush canopy, provided shade and a sense of tranquility. The missionary residence would be constructed from local timber and boast a design that harmonized with the surrounding environment. It would feature spacious verandas overlooking the river, allowing residents to take in the serene vistas. The interior would be designed for comfort, with well-ventilated rooms that invited the gentle breeze of the river. Nearby, nestled amid the trees, the schools would be located. These would be designed with both practicality and aesthetics in mind. Classrooms, with their large windows, would allow natural light to flood in, creating an inviting space for learning. The outdoor areas would be expansive, offering plenty of room for students to play, explore, and find inspiration in the embrace of nature.

The combination of scenic beauty and comfortable infrastructure was intended to create an environment where spiritual and academic growth could flourish. The missionaries believed that the harmonious surroundings would encourage a sense of wonder and curiosity among the students, fostering a deep connection with the land and the teachings of faith. And so, they began the construction. As the missionaries embarked on constructing their envisioned residence and schools, they encountered many challenges.

The scarcity of skilled labor presented a significant hurdle, as finding enough experienced workers who were well-versed in construction proved to be a daunting task. They opted to have construction methods that were similar to those that were already used in the tribe. However, they wanted to use some of the newer Western-style methods that gave foundations a more solid base, making the walls more durable.

Therefore, the workers who did join and work for them were at times confused and found it difficult to work according to the new instructions. Moreover, the mission faced challenges such as the theft of construction materials, causing delays and financial strain. They did not know who was stealing the materials and equipment, so they attempted to lock away the equipment in a makeshift shed at night and have someone stand guard at all times.

Unpredictable weather patterns added to their woes, as torrential rains sometimes hindered progress. This, coupled with a lack of modern construction machinery, meant that much of the work had to be done manually, with shovels and hand tools. Additionally, a lack of reliable transportation infrastructure made the transportation of building materials a logistical challenge. Therefore, the construction took a lot of time. They knew Satan would do all he could to stop the building of the mission and the school. He would seek to destroy their work and test their resilience. They had learned from **Luke 22-23**, the story from the last moments of Jesus' life, that Satan intensely and intentionally opposes what God is doing in this world. They knew that, as missionaries, they would be under attack. In **1 Peter 5:8**, Peter warns the believers who are under persecution to be on the alert because our *"adversary the devil prowls around like a roaring lion, seeking someone to devour."*

In other words, Satan wants to tear us to pieces as well. Like a lion in its natural habitat, he sits back and looks for the vulnerable and weak so that he might devour his prey. ***Ephesians 6:10-12*** underscores this battle as well. Our battle is not against *"flesh and blood"* but rather against *"the rulers, against the authorities, against the cosmic powers over this present darkness, against the spiritual forces of evil in the heavenly places."*

Verse 13 adds that we are to take up the armor so that we can withstand *"in the evil day."* Verse 16 encourages us to take our shield in order to *"extinguish all the flaming darts of the evil one."* They were in a battle daily but understood that victory would come with faith.

The mission was resolute, and they began their preaching immediately despite a lack of shelter and infrastructure. They had brought with them some standing chalkboards and a mountain of books on the Gospel and other teachings. They used these to teach the children and people by taking their supplies to a nearby field and having the people sit with them in a circle on the ground. They did not get far as the people were still weary of them, but these interactions served as a good starting point and a way to let the people know what the mission was about and how it would be sharing the Gospel and the teachings of Christ.

Issues of cultural understanding occasionally arose with these learners and with the local craftsmen and laborers. Effective communication and mutual respect were essential to bridge any gaps in understanding and ensure the smooth progression of the project. Despite these challenges, the missionaries remained resolute in realizing their vision. They saw each obstacle as an opportunity for growth in terms of their faith and understanding of the land and its people. Their determination and unwavering faith in their mission fortified their resolve to overcome the challenges they faced in building a place of spiritual and educational enrichment in the heart of Mende.

As the construction of the missionary residence and schools continued, interactions unfolded between Ann, the other missionaries, and the native children and adults who frequented the construction site. The presence of children was a constant source of joy and curiosity, and Ann, in particular, found herself drawn to them. Overpowering the sounds of hammering and sawing, the laughter of children became a melody that echoed through the construction site. Ann would often sit with a group of wide-eyed youngsters, their bare feet grounded in the red earth. She would teach them songs, sharing the uplifting hymns of faith that had traveled across the ocean with her. Their voices, harmonizing in the Sherbro language, formed a chorus of hope.

The children were quick to reciprocate, teaching Ann the nuances of their own language and the names of the vibrant flora that surrounded them. The Raymond's children often joined Ann during these times and became fast friends with the Mende children. These exchanges displayed the universality of childhood wonder and the transcendent power of shared laughter. The words of her Savior echoed in her mind.

"Let the little children come to Me, and do not forbid them; for of such is the kingdom of heaven."

– Matthew 19:14

The adults who visited the site were equally intrigued by the missionaries and their purpose. Conversations flowed freely as they toiled alongside the missionaries, offering their labor and expertise. The language barrier was bridged with gestures, shared smiles, and the universal language of human connection. Ann, with her radiant spirit, became a bridge between cultures, her genuine curiosity fostering a sense of camaraderie. She listened intently to the stories shared by the native adults, learning about their traditions, their families, and their dreams for the future. Through these interactions, the bonds of friendship and mutual respect deepened, creating a sense of unity among the labor and toil.

Once the construction dust had settled and the final touches had been added, the missionary residence and schools stood as beacons of hope and proof of the magnificent work of the Lord in the heart of Mende. The home, nestled in the lush greenery and overlooking the serene river, embodied the harmonious integration of faith and nature.

The residence featured a wide, welcoming veranda adorned with vibrant flowers, providing a serene space for contemplation. The interior exuded warmth, with polished wooden floors and handcrafted furnishings that bore witness to the local craftsmanship. Each room was illuminated by the soft glow of sunlight streaming through large windows.

The schools situated nearby were a vision of educational promise. Spacious classrooms, flooded with natural light, provided an inviting atmosphere for learning.

Colorful educational materials adorned the walls, offering a visual feast for young minds eager to explore. Many of the paintings hung on the walls were created by the children of Mende, forming a gallery that showcased how the mission was encouraging the creativity and the spiritual learning of the people. The expansive outdoor areas were adorned with shade-giving trees, offering students ample space to play, learn, and connect with the land that had given them their unique heritage.

The completed structures served as places of spiritual growth and academic enrichment and as symbols of unity between the missionaries and the community. The vibrant flora surrounding them reminded them of the harmonious relationship between faith and the natural world, nurturing both the spirit and intellect of those who sought knowledge and solace within their walls.

Even though the main focus was the people of Mende and fostering a connection with them, the bonds between the mission members themselves were also strengthened during this time. Within the bustling sounds of construction and the harmonious laughter of children, there existed a unique bond between Daddy George and Ann, a bond forged in faith and kindred spirits.

Daddy George, known by all as the steadfast coxswain and a devout Christian, was a pillar of strength within the missionary community.

His unwavering devotion to God and the mission resonated deeply with Ann, and a profound respect blossomed between them. It was a relationship akin to a spiritual mentor and a devoted disciple. Their conversations often revolved around matters of faith, with Daddy George frequently visiting Ann's room for discussions that delved into the depths of the Gospel.

These moments were more than just words; they were the exchange of souls seeking a greater understanding of God's divine plan. They explored the intricacies of Scripture, shared passages that had touched their hearts, and reflected on the teachings of Jesus Christ.

Ann would listen intently as Daddy George, with the wisdom of years spent walking in faith, shared his insights and interpretations of the Gospel.

His words were a source of spiritual nourishment, enriching her understanding of God's boundless love and grace. It was in these conversations that Ann's faith flourished, growing stronger with each passing day.

Their connection went beyond theological discussions, with the two sharing stories about their lives, families, values, hopes, and dreams. It showed the genuine concern and care that Daddy George held for Ann.

In the privacy of her room, he would offer heartfelt prayers on her behalf, beseeching the Lord to *"have mercy upon little sister Ann."*

His petitions were not mere words but a reflection of a deep and abiding love for a fellow believer. With each prayer, he implored the Almighty to build her up in the most holy faith and grant her strength amid the afflictions that had touched her body. Ann had become sickly while in Mende due to the change in the air and the newness of the foods and drinks that the land and the people offered them. Therefore, there was an earnestness in George's words, a sincerity that emanated from a heart that genuinely cared for Ann's well-being.

These moments of prayer and conversation displayed the depth of their bond. The mission knew that the two were becoming fast friends and had a mentor/mentee connection.

Daddy George, with his wife, Mommy Mary, became an integral part of Ann's spiritual journey.

Their faith-filled discussions not only fortified Ann's resolve but also served as a reminder that they were not alone in their mission. They were united by their shared devotion to God and the unwavering belief that they were instruments of His divine purpose.

As time went on, Daddy George and Ann continued their conversations of faith, their voices echoing through the mission, a presentation of the enduring power of shared beliefs and the unbreakable bonds of spiritual family.

While forging a connection between the mission members was easy, connecting with the natives proved a much more difficult task, one that required guidance from the Lord. The missionaries knew that their mission was clear: to convince the people of Mende to embrace the schools and teachings they offered.

However, this endeavor was no easy task, as it was rooted in deeply ingrained fears, cultural differences, and the clash of belief systems.

While the previous setup of teaching on the floor in the open was not as formidable, the new large structures and the disciple and curated method that the mission had now started employing made the natives of Mende more apprehensive about their desires. Like many African communities of that era, the people of Mende held a deep-seated apprehension toward White foreigners.

The arrival of the missionaries from the Western world stirred a sense of unease among the native population. The unfamiliarity with their customs, language, and beliefs cast a long shadow of suspicion over their interactions.

The Western beliefs propagated by the missionaries posed a direct challenge to the traditional religion and spiritual practices of the Mende people. Their spirituality was ingrained into their existence, and the prospect of embracing foreign ideologies was met with trepidation.

The mere thought of veering away from their ancestral traditions was akin to breaking sacred bonds nurtured through generations. Oral tradition had been the bedrock of knowledge transmission for the Mende people. The concept of books and written texts was a novel and bewildering concept. The written word held an aura of mystique, and many viewed it with a mixture of fascination and fear. It was as if the pages held a power that could disrupt the delicate equilibrium of their lives. Faced with these formidable hurdles, the missionaries turned to diplomacy and understanding. They recognized that building bridges required patience and respect for the rich cultural heritage of Mende. It was not enough to simply preach; they needed to listen, learn, and adapt.

The turning point came with the support of the Tribe's king. He had spent time with the missionaries, understanding their intentions and witnessing the transformation of the local children who attended the mission's schools. The king, with his deep sense of responsibility toward his people, began to advocate for the mission.

He urged families to come and hear the word, to allow their children to study in these foreign schools. His influence was significant, as his word carried immense weight among the Mende people. Slowly but surely, families began to tentatively step forward, placing their trust in the missionaries. However, the challenges persisted. The people of Mende harbored a deep-seated fear of White foreigners, which had been exacerbated by the exploitation and abuse faced by European colonizers. The legacy of colonialism loomed large, casting a dark shadow over the prospect of accepting Western teachings. Furthermore, the beliefs and practices of the Mende people were deeply intertwined with their daily lives. Their spirituality was not confined to a place of worship; it permeated every aspect of their existence. To embrace Christianity meant challenging age-old traditions and customs, a prospect that stirred anxiety and resistance. The missionaries also grappled with the vast chasm of language and communication. The Mende people spoke a language foreign to the missionaries, and the absence of a common tongue made meaningful dialogue a significant hurdle. Translation efforts were often fraught with misunderstandings, and the nuances of faith and theology were challenging to convey accurately despite the help of the Amistad. Yet, despite these formidable obstacles, the missionaries remained steadfast in their commitment. They believed in the transformative power of education and faith and approached their mission with unwavering determination. To address the prevailing fears, the missionaries took deliberate steps to demystify their presence.

They invited members of the community to their gatherings and schools, fostering an environment of openness and trust. By sharing meals and engaging in daily life alongside the Mende people, they sought to break down the barriers that had separated them.

Over time, the missionaries worked tirelessly to build bridges of understanding. They respected the Mende way of life, incorporating elements of the local culture into their teachings. This approach helped to dispel some of the initial fears and apprehensions.

The king's endorsement and personal interactions with the missionaries were a great help. His influence carried immense weight, as his role as a spiritual and community leader was pivotal. He often spoke to the people who were apprehensive directly and convinced them to give the mission a try. He had seen firsthand the positive impact of education and faith on other tribes and wanted the same for his people.

The missionaries felt renewed hope and gratitude for each family that chose to join the mission. Their struggles had not been in vain. The seeds of faith and education had taken root in the hearts of the Mende people, and the mission was beginning to bear fruit. Over time, children who had once viewed books with trepidation now embraced them with curiosity and enthusiasm. Families began to recognize that the mission offered opportunities for their children that would shape their futures. The missionaries' unwavering dedication to education and faith had started yielding results. They discovered profound fulfillment in their divine labor.

They had triumphed over formidable obstacles, knitting bonds of trust and Christian fellowship with the souls they had been summoned to minister unto. Though the journey remained lengthy and beset with trials, they traversed it, guided by the radiant light of the conviction that they were effecting profound transformation, one family, one soul at a time. The words of hope and eternal salvation were gradually finding sanctuary within the hearts of the people of Mende.

The missionaries, infused with an unwavering sense of divine purpose and the Holy Spirit, pressed onward in their noble crusade to bridge the earthly chasm and share the eternal Word of God.

Chapter 6: Our Hope

The memory of the first time Ann caught fever remained etched in her mind and the minds of her loved ones like a haunting refrain. It was a day seared with the intensity of the African sun, a scorching heat that bore down upon her with unrelenting force. She had embarked on this mission with a heart full of conviction, ready to serve God in the distant land of Sierra Leone. But on this particular day, her resolve was tested as she felt the onset of her fever's cruel grip. The fever crept upon her like an uninvited guest, its insidious presence making itself known through chills that wracked her body and a relentless ache that settled deep within her bones. As she lay in her humble quarters, beads of perspiration formed on her brow, and her once steady hands trembled with weakness.

Despite the overwhelming fatigue and the unyielding fever, Ann clung to her faith with unwavering determination. She believed that God had called her to this mission, and no amount of suffering would deter her from fulfilling that divine purpose. In her solitude, she whispered prayers, seeking solace and strength with trust in the Almighty God. Exhausted and racked with pain, she uttered these words through parched and cracked lips:

"Father God, today I come before you in full recognition and praise for your power and love. You are our true source for healing and wholeness in all aspects of my life. In Your

mercy, I ask for physical healing, that You would touch and mend every aspect of my body that is in need. Grant me strength and vitality that I may experience Your healing touch in every cell and fiber of my being. Return to me the strength I need to carry on the mission you have given me. O Holy God, stretch out your healing hand, I pray, Amen."

Her day, once filled with the fervor of mission work, now revolved around the small acts of survival. The simple task of rising from her bed became a monumental effort, but Ann pressed on. She found solace in the voices of the African natives who offered their guidance and remedies.

The locals had become a source of support and companionship for her, sharing their knowledge of indigenous herbs and natural remedies. They believed in the healing power of the land and its ability to provide relief from afflictions. Hoping to alleviate Ann's suffering, they concocted herbal infusions and poultices.

As the fever ebbed and flowed, Ann experienced moments of respite. She watched the world outside her window, African life that continued to unfold. The laughter of children playing, the rhythmic beat of drums in the distance, and the bustling marketplaces were all reminders that life in Sierra Leone persisted, even in the face of illness. Through it all, Ann maintained her unwavering resolve. She saw her illness as a test of her faith, a challenge placed before her by God. She believed that God would relieve her suffering in time, and this steadfast conviction carried her through the darkest hours of her fever. One of her favorite Scriptures, Psalm 23, had helped her through difficult times. In moments of solitude as she lay in her bed, she would bring it to mind and pray:

"The Lord is my shepherd; I shall not want. He maketh me to lie down in green pastures: he leadeth me beside the still waters. He restoreth my soul: he leadeth me in the paths of righteousness for his name's sake. Yea, though I walk through the valley of the shadow of death, I will fear no evil: for thou art with me; thy rod and thy staff they comfort me. Thou preparest a table before me in the presence of mine enemies: thou anointest my head with oil; my cup runneth over. Surely goodness and mercy shall follow me all the days of my life: and I will dwell in the house of the Lord forever."

-Psalm 23

Ann discovered an enduring wellspring of strength within the warm embrace of the African community that had welcomed her as kin. With tenderness, they handed her cups of herbal infusions brewed from leaves and roots, each sip a testament to their care. They whispered words of encouragement, their voices a soothing balm to her weary soul. Their eyes, filled with empathy, met hers, conveying an unspoken promise of shared burdens. These kind-hearted people provided her with reassurance that transcended language barriers. In their presence, Ann felt the palpable embrace of their community, a testament to the depth of their love. It was a love that transcended culture and continents and affirmed her place among them. Their guidance extended beyond remedies as they shared stories of resilience and survival, tales of ancestors who had weathered storms and emerged stronger.

No one offered her more support and care than William Raymond, her father figure and mentor. He helped her much during this ordeal, along with his caring and loving wife, Mrs. Raymond. The benevolent presence of the Raymonds, like guardian angels, offered her solace and care that transcended the physical realm.

Mr. Raymond, with his boundless grace and firm strength, assumed the role of Ann's dedicated caretaker. He became both a physician and nurse, providing for her in a land where medical resources were scarce and rudimentary. His presence was a source of great comfort to Ann, for she trusted him implicitly, knowing that his care was driven by deep compassion and faith. Each day, Mr. Raymond would sit by Ann's side, offering her soothing words of encouragement and prayers that soared heavenward. He assured her that God's watchful eye was upon her and that this trial, though formidable, was but a fleeting moment in her mission. He would read scriptures to her and pray with her each morning and evening. Both of them found great comfort and hope in God's Word.

Mrs. Raymond, no less compassionate, attended to Ann with tenderness and affection. She would place cool, damp cloths upon Ann's feverish forehead, offering respite from the oppressive heat. Her gentle touch was a balm to Ann's weary soul, a reminder that she was not alone in her suffering.

In their modest kitchen, the Raymonds labored to prepare nourishing meals, especially crafted to aid Ann's recovery. Each dish had the imprint of their love and devotion, for in this foreign land, they had become Ann's surrogate family.

The fever raged on for days, its intensity at times alarming. Yet, compared to the severe cases that often plagued missionaries in these lands, Ann's affliction was relatively mild. Nevertheless, her strength waned, and she lay bedridden for a better part of ten days.

Amidst Ann's fevered dreams and fitful nights, the Raymonds' voices rose in fervent prayer, seeking divine intervention and healing.

Their unwavering faith served as a beacon of hope, reminding Ann that even in the darkest of times, God's light would shine through. Once, a place of worship and refuge, the mission house was transformed into a sanctuary for Ann's recovery. It echoed with the hymns of faith and the whispered words of comfort, a display of the strength of their shared devotion.

As the days stretched into weeks, Ann's fever gradually began to recede. The unwavering support, the heartfelt prayers, and the loving care of Mr. and Mrs. Raymond had seen her through this trying ordeal.

Their presence had been a profound expression of God's love, a tangible reminder that in the service of their divine calling, they were bound not only by faith but by the deepest bonds of compassion and family.

As the fever eventually broke and Ann's strength returned, she emerged from her ordeal with a profound sense of resilience.

She knew that the road ahead would be fraught with challenges, but she also understood that her faith would be her guiding light. The first encounter with fever had tested her, but it had not broken her. Ann stood ready to face whatever trials lay ahead, fortified by her unshakable belief in the mission and Almighty God.

The day Ann emerged from the mission home and stepped into the warm African sun, the Mende joined in shouts or praise and dancing. Their Ann had returned. Although still weak, she joined in the celebration. An impromptu time of worship and thanksgiving was led by Mr. and Mrs. Raymond. However, their trials and tribulations were not yet over. In the sweltering embrace of Sierra Leone's tropical climate, the missionaries faced a relentless test of faith. The next one to succumb to illness was Mrs. Raymond's infant son and then her.

Mrs. Raymond had given birth to a son, a joyous occasion that had brought hope and light to their mission house. Everyone was overjoyed with the arrival of her baby boy.

This new life was a wonderful gift to all. They looked to God and gave thanks, seeing this as a blessing and affirmation of their work here in Mende. Ann was nearly as excited over the coming of a child into the mission as his parents were.

Children had always been dear to her heart, and this one would bring such joy to the family, the mission, and the community.

When the baby was just 10 days old, they brought him down to the river for his baptism. It looked like a mini-safari as neighbors, mission folk, and of course, the king walked down to witness the special occasion.

What a joyous day it was, a great celebration as children danced and women sang. Once at the river, Mr. Raymond, with his white shirt and khaki slacks, waded into the river with little George in his arms. Mrs. Raymond watched lovingly from the water's edge. Her husband lifted their child high into the air and prayed:

"We thank you, almighty God, for the gift of water to sustain, refresh, and cleanse all life. Over water, the Holy

Spirit moved in the beginning of creation. Through water, you led the children of Israel from slavery in Egypt to freedom in the Promised Land. In water, your Son Jesus received the baptism of John and was anointed by the Holy Spirit as the Messiah, the Christ, to lead us from the death of sin to newness of life. We thank you, Father, for the water of baptism; in it, we are buried with Christ in His death; by it, we share in His resurrection. Amen."

He then lowered baby George down under the water and out again. All those watching shouted with excitement, and many jumped for joy. Mr. Raymond returned his son to his mother's arms and began to step out of the water only to be confronted with a number of Mende, young and old, who desired to be baptized. That day, 20 members of the tribe accepted Christ as their Savior and were baptized in His name.

However, this happiness would soon turn to grief, as their infant son's life was cut tragically short after just five weeks. The illness had been brief. At first, he seemed a little warm, but then the fever overtook his tiny body, and he went into seizures.

They did everything they could, but it was not to be God's will for the child to survive. Ann spent hours on her knees pleading with God to heal the child. She even tried bargaining with God, asking that He take her life instead. When the news came that little George had gone to heaven, she wept for hours. The loss was profound and cast a pall over the entire mission. The missionaries, who had come to view each other as a second family in this distant land, rallied around the Raymonds in their time of sorrow. The communal bonds of faith and friendship served as a source of solace as they navigated the painful aftermath of this heartbreaking loss.

Mrs. Raymond, already weakened by her health issues, was deeply affected by the loss of her child. The grief was an indescribable burden, weighing heavily upon her fragile frame. Her husband, Mr. Raymond, found himself grappling with the immense sorrow that had descended upon their household. With its noble purpose and determined faith, the mission they had embarked upon had now confronted them with the harsh reality of mortality.

The loss of the Raymonds' infant son reverberated throughout the mission house. Ann, who had grown close to the Raymonds and cherished their friendship, felt the profound sadness that enveloped their home.

Her youthful heart ached as she witnessed the grief that engulfed her missionary companions, and she, too, sought comfort in the shared faith that bound them together. At first, Ann and Mr. Raymond would offer up prayers and read scriptures together. There, they found comfort and peace. The pain was too great, and Mrs. Raymond stayed in her room. Tears of pain and sorrow streamed down her face until sleep overtook her. Her dreams were filled with visions of her tiny son. She would wake up thinking it was all a dream, only to be broken again by the reality of her loss. It would be many days before she ventured out and joined her husband and Ann.

The loss of the child, while devastating, deepened the resolve of the Raymonds and the entire missionary community.

They clung to their faith with renewed determination, believing that even in the face of profound sorrow, their mission was guided by a greater purpose. Their commitment to sharing the Word of God with the people of Sierra Leone remained resolute, and they moved forward, strengthened by the shared bond of faith that had sustained them through their darkest hours. Yet it seemed that Sierra Leone, with its unforgiving environment, was exacting a heavy toll on newcomers.

Mrs. Raymond, weakened by the trials of childbirth, soon succumbed to a fever that wracked her body with unrelenting intensity. The missionaries, including Ann, could only watch with heavy hearts as she battled this relentless affliction, fully aware that their medical resources were limited.

As the weeks wore on, hope for Mrs. Raymond's recovery waned. The loss of her infant son after a mere five weeks left a profound scar on her soul. The joyous arrival seemed to have been cruelly eclipsed by a swift and sorrowful departure, casting a long shadow of grief over the family and the entire mission. The burden of this tragedy extended beyond Mrs. Raymond. The death of an innocent infant challenged the core of the mission's faith, a stark reminder that their missionary path was fraught with sacrifice.

Ann, who had come to view her fellow missionaries as a second family, was deeply affected by the unfolding events. Her youthful optimism faced a stern test, and she grappled with the harsh realities of their chosen path. The loss was a stark reminder that their mission was not without its share of sorrows and that even the most faithful were not immune to heartache.

The Raymond children, too, felt the weight of their parents' distress. They observed with concern as their mother's health continued to deteriorate, their youthful innocence contrasting sharply with the gravity of their worries.

The vibrant landscape, once filled with the promise of a new season, now seemed tinged with unfamiliar sadness. As the African rains loomed on the horizon, a palpable shift in the atmosphere took hold. The air, thick with humidity, pressed down upon the mission house like an oppressive shroud. Once parched and cracked, the landscape revealed signs of impending transformation, with dark clouds gathering ominously on the horizon. In the face of these trials, Ann and Mr. Raymond remained unwavering. They understood that their mission was not solely defined by its hardships but by their unyielding commitment to their calling.

Their path, fraught with difficulties, mirrored the unpredictable nature of life itself. Soon after, Ann found herself ensnared by the clutches of fever once again. The relentless cycles of illness and recovery had become an unwelcome rhythm in her missionary journey. This time, the fever was accompanied by a sinister duo—inflammation and constipation, turning her frailty into a fierce adversary.

The fever's onset was a gradual descent into discomfort. Ann, acutely attuned to her body after enduring previous bouts of illness, recognized the initial signs all too well. It began with a subtle malaise, an unsettling sensation that whispered of impending affliction. Fatigue crept over her like a heavy shroud, leaving her drained and listless.

Her limbs ached, and a persistent chill gnawed at her core despite the oppressive heat that hung in the air. As the fever tightened its grip, inflammation set in, intensifying her misery.

Her body felt as if it were at war with itself, each joint and muscle protesting with fiery agony. She struggled to find respite, her restless nights filled with fitful sleep and feverish dreams. The beads of sweat that formed on her brow did little to quell the relentless heat that coursed through her veins.

The inflammation was accompanied by an insidious companion—constipation. Her abdomen became a battleground of discomfort, bloated and unyielding. The simple act of eating, once a source of sustenance and pleasure, had now become a torment. Ann longed for relief, both from the oppressive fever and the internal struggle that waged within her.

In the grip of fever, Ann found herself wrestling not only with physical affliction but also the pangs of fear. The oppressive heat of Sierra Leone bore down upon her frail form, and in moments of vulnerability, a sense of trepidation loomed large. It was in these hours of isolation and illness that her heart ached most for the comforting presence of her mother, a beacon of love and solace she had left far behind.

As the fever raged within her, Ann's thoughts often wandered to her distant home, where the gentle embrace of her mother had been a refuge in times of trouble.

The longing for that reassuring touch, the soothing words only a mother could offer, was an ache that penetrated her soul. Amid unfamiliar faces and an alien landscape, Ann felt a profound sense of homesickness, a yearning for the maternal warmth she had known all her life. The fears that gripped her were multifaceted—a fear of the unknown, of the relentless African weather, of the formidable illnesses that seemed to haunt her path. Yet, the fear that cut deepest was the fear of being alone in a foreign land, far from the comforting presence of her mother. It was a fear that whispered in the darkest recesses of her heart, a constant reminder of the immense sacrifice she had made in answering God's call.

As Ann lay in her modest quarters, seeking relief from the fever, she drew strength from the shared faith of her missionary companions.

Mr. Raymond, who had been her anchor in times of trouble, offered her comforting words and fervent prayers for her recovery. Together, they sought divine intervention, believing God's mercy would ultimately prevail.

Ann believed that her suffering held a purpose, a testament to her steady commitment to the mission and her trust in God's plan. Her thoughts turned to the people of Sierra Leone, many of whom faced similar trials daily. Ann's own affliction allowed her to empathize with their plight and fostered a deeper connection to the community she had come to serve.

The African natives, who had embraced her as one of their own, recognized Ann's suffering and once again offered their remedies with compassion and kindness. They brewed herbal concoctions, hoping to ease her discomfort. Their words of reassurance, spoken in a language foreign to her but understood in the language of empathy, provided a measure of solace.

In the face of adversity, Ann's determination remained unbroken. She had come to Sierra Leone with a purpose, a divine calling that transcended the challenges of illness. Her missionary journey, fraught with hardships and trials, was a testament to her unwavering commitment to spreading the Word of God.

Even as fever, inflammation, and constipation sought to hinder her path, Ann's faith burned brightly, a beacon of resilience in the midst of adversity.

Throughout this harrowing chapter in their missionary journey, Mr. Raymond emerged as a steadfast pillar of support, revealing the depths of his compassion and devotion.

While Ann grappled with her recurring fever and illness, and Mrs. Raymond was sick, mourning the loss of their infant son, it was Mr. Raymond who shouldered the weight of their collective suffering.

With inspiring grace and unyielding strength, he took on the dual roles of caregiver and comforter. His love for Ann, whom he had come to regard as a spiritual daughter, and for his ailing wife was boundless. In the sweltering heat of Sierra Leone, Mr. Raymond assumed the role of physician, tending to Ann's needs as best he could.

He became her devoted nurse again, tirelessly attending to her throughout her feverish bouts and moments of despair. Cooling cloths were gently placed upon her fevered brow, and he ensured she received nourishing food to regain her strength. His actions were not just the duties of a caretaker but the gestures of a compassionate father figure, offering solace through his presence and reassuring words. In those trying times, his prayers for Ann's recovery were fervent, a testament to the depth of his concern. As Mr. Raymond tended to Ann, his heart bore the weight of personal grief.

The loss of his five-week-old son was a devastating blow, and though he pushed his sorrow aside to care for others, the pain he carried was a burden only he truly understood. His quiet moments of reflection were filled with longing for the child he had lost and the anguish of watching his wife's health deteriorate. Despite the trials that threatened to engulf him, Mr. Raymond remained steadfast in his faith. He found solace in the knowledge that their mission was a divine calling, a purpose that transcended personal suffering.

The spiritual bond he shared with Ann and his wife deepened through their collective struggles, reinforcing their commitment to the work they had undertaken. Yet, even in his unwavering faith, there were moments of fear and doubt. He feared that God, in His mysterious plan, might call Ann and his beloved wife to heaven, leaving him to continue the mission alone. The prospect of such a loss weighed heavily on his heart, a testament to his profound love for the two women who were his family in this distant land.

Chapter 7: Pressing Forward

Ann's afflictions originated back in New York, where she faced her first health challenge since leaving her home in Haverhill. Growing up, she had battled fatigue and other maladies that left as quickly as they had come on her. This time, it manifested as a severe cold. She thought it may have been due to the change in climate or an allergic reaction to something she ate. Dismissed it as a passing ailment at the time, unaware that it marked the beginning of her physical trials. To her, it was a fleeting cold, vanishing without leaving a lasting imprint.

However, the pattern of her fragile health soon became apparent. The ship's journey to Mende had brought another wave of illness, this time as persistent constipation. Ann resorted to regular doses of medication to find relief, determined to persist on her path, guided by her unwavering faith in Christ. She pressed forward, her spirit unbroken.

Upon arriving in York, another fever had besieged her, exacerbated by her digestive issues. She had hoped that she had outgrown the digestive problems that her physician had diagnosed when she was in her early teens. Yet, in the face of these physical tribulations, Ann clung to her steadfast resolve to fully embrace her new mission and walk the path illuminated by Christ's guidance.

Her health saw a temporary respite after this fever subsided, and Ann enjoyed a semblance of well-being for a while. However, when the mission reached Kaw Mende, history repeated itself. Once again, the familiar sequence unfolded, and the fever returned, accompanied by her recurrent abdominal troubles.

Through these recurring trials, Ann's faith remained unwavering, a beacon of strength that helped her navigate the unpredictable waters of her health. These physical afflictions marked her journey, but her determination to serve her higher purpose and follow Christ's call never wavered. In early May, a distressing affliction seized Ann's stomach, tormenting her for nearly an agonizing hour. With Mr. Raymond so busy with the work of the mission, Mrs. Raymond, deeply concerned, administered various remedies commonly employed for colic, yet the relief they brought proved fleeting. At Ann's request, a potent elixir of cayenne pepper tea was prescribed, and to her great relief, it worked like a miracle, soothing her suffering stomach. However, the lingering consequences persisted, and her once-resilient stomach seemed permanently altered. Though the intensity had somewhat waned, it became a source of frequent discomfort. Then came the fateful Monday, May 20th, when the treacherous specter of bowel inflammation descended upon her. The gravity of the situation was unmistakable. Mrs. Raymond, fueled by unwavering determination, immediately sprang into action. She applied a blistering poultice with precision, a steadfast attempt to wrestle the malady into submission. It clung for close to twenty-four hours, but alas, the relentless tropical climate had robbed the plaster of its potency.

Unfazed, she turned to an equally fervent mustard poultice, meticulously applying it over the same vital area. This time, it yielded the desired outcome. Gradually, the suffocating grip of inflammation released its hold, granting Ann the precious gift of relief. Yet, as is often the case with such trials, it exacted a toll—a weariness that coursed through her body, leaving her physically spent.

As the sun dipped below the horizon on Sunday, the 26th, Ann's condition had grown alarmingly feeble. Through the silent hours of the night, Mr. Raymond, in from his work at the mission, stood vigilant, lifting her gently each time she sought solace in a sip of cool water.

It was during this time, amid the darkness, that Mrs. Raymod began to display the unmistakable signs of impending labor. Mr. Raymond's heart, already burdened by the fear of her prior severe fever, now raced with fresh concern. Remarkably, despite her profound weakness, Ann summoned up reserves of courage and determination she might not have known she possessed. With a resilient spirit forged by unwavering faith, she rose from her weakened state, meticulously dressing herself, and went to be with Mrs. Raymond through her labor. The strength and courage that

Ann displayed in that moment was astounding and was most certainly enabled through God's divine grace. God blessed Mr. Raymond with a respite and a chance to feel the happiness of a new child. A new life entered the world in the early morning of that fateful Monday. The baby's first cries, a chorus of hope, echoed through the room. Ann, with the gentle touch of a mother and the tenderness of a saint, cradled the newborn, cleansing and swaddling it herself.

It was proof of her unyielding spirit, a reminder that even in the depths of suffering, a mother's love and a missionary's resolve could persevere. As the profound act of nurturing concluded, Ann's strength was wholly spent, and she sank, profoundly exhausted, onto the bed.

On the next day, Mrs. Raymond yearned to perform the simple act of dressing the baby, her heart heavy with the weight of her own incapacity.

It was Ann who gently took the infant in her arms, an act of kindness that spoke volumes of her unwavering devotion. The child was swathed in the gentle folds of her care, each movement showing Ann's compassionate spirit. Yet, the night descended with an eerie warning. Ann, in the clutches of a malady resembling palsy, found herself robbed of control over her limbs as if a shadow had fallen over her strength. As the sun rose on Wednesday, Mrs. Raymond, already weakened by her prior tribulations, was assailed by a violent onslaught of diarrhea.

Her body, once vibrant with life, lay now in complete surrender, mirroring the vulnerability of an infant. This was the time when Mr. Raymond stood alone, grappling with the enormity of the responsibilities — two helpless women and a newborn baby depended on him for their most basic needs.

The weight of this burden was unparalleled, perhaps the heaviest ever bestowed upon him by the Heavenly Father. His hands became the hands of a caretaker, washing, dressing, and feeding with a tender precision born of necessity. Three days later, Mrs. Raymond's health reached a level so dire that she and her husband feared the specter of a grim and unrelenting fate. In a poignant farewell, she summoned her children to her side, their hearts heavy with the foreboding of finality. However, at approximately four o'clock that day, a divine intervention occurred. The fever relinquished its hold, and the relentless diarrhea abated. With astounding swiftness, she regained her strength, to the astonishment of all. Mr. Raymond, the children, and their mother grasped hands and, looking heavenward, joined in prayer, Mr. Raymond leading:

"Our Father who art in heaven hallowed be thy name. They kingdom come thy will be done on earth as it is in heaven. Give us this day our daily bread and forgive us our trespasses as we forgive those who trespass against us and lead us not into temptation but deliver us form evil, for thine is the kingdom and the power and the glory for ever and ever. Amen"

Mr. Raymond and the whole family rose to their feet, and with their hands lifted high they sang,

"Praise God from whom all blessings flow, Praise Him all creatures here below, Praise Him above, ye heavenly hosts, Praise Father Son and Holy Ghost. Amen."

Two days later, she was resolute in her desire to nurse the child, a testament to her enduring maternal love. It was a beautiful and heartrending gesture, for she nursed the infant with a fervor that belied her frailty. One week passed in this tender embrace, but as her strength waned, she was left utterly depleted. Ann, having herself found strength anew, took the child into her own care. Although Mr. Raymond offered to shoulder the responsibility, she insisted, arguing that his already heavy load should not be compounded.

Ann cared for the child with a devotion that knew no bounds. Her resilience was commendable, yet it was not without its price. Eventually, the relentless march of time carried them to the first of July, when the Lord called the little one unto Himself, to a realm free of earthly afflictions. An event that ripped through the entire mission and left all with a profound feeling of sadness and loss.

Throughout these trials, Ann's indomitable spirit wrestled with the chains of obstinate constipation, interspersed with bouts of violent vomiting and recurring tremors resembling palsy. Her affliction followed a peculiar pattern that shadowed her steps and tested her faith in the most trying of ways. In those disconcerting days, whenever Ann endeavored to employ her hand, an unsettling tremor would consume her, causing her limbs to convulse erratically. These involuntary movements persisted for minutes on end, rendering her limbs utterly uncooperative. A simple act, like raising a cup to her lips to quench her thirst, became a formidable challenge. Her head would sway, propelled by these sudden and uncontrollable motions, until it hung low as if bereft of strength. Through sheer determination and unwavering support, Mr. Raymond administered water to her. Nestled in her bed, she lacked the strength to sit upright unaided. With tender care, he positioned her and held her close, offering water drop by precious drop. In those days of infirmity, tasks as mundane as personal grooming became monumental feats. The simple acts of washing and combing her hair eluded her for an extended period. It was Mr. Raymond who attended to these humble yet crucial needs. Ann's condition fluctuated unpredictably. There were moments when her power of speech would inexplicably vanish, rendering her mute. At times, her senses seemed dulled, as though she dwelled in a realm separate from the world around her.

The unyielding grip of constipation compounded her suffering. Relief was fleeting, and Ann's stomach rejected almost everything it received. Mr. Raymond, in his steadfast dedication, exhausted every means to alleviate her torment.

He searched for solutions, but the unforgiving nature of the sickness defied remedy. Laxatives proved impractical, given the complexities of administering them, and propriety stood in the way of other options. This affliction, mysterious in origin, eventually relinquished its hold, but not without its toll. Ann's once-keen mind bore scars, marked by moments of incomprehensible stupor and occasional obsessions. At this point, Mr. Raymond decided to have a caretaker come to look after Ann for all hours of the day. The name of the girl was Maria, and the two soon became close, with Maria showing Ann intense empathy and understanding while Ann found a companion and solace in Maria. She was so close to the girl that she would always call out to her first thing in the morning. Maria never left Ann's side and showed her great grace and compassion, as Ann had shown the people of Mende while she was well.

Soon after, the mission members all moved to the mission house, which had been being built while they stayed in makeshift spaces. Ann, Mr. Raymond, and Mrs. Raymond all moved to the new mission house in Kaw Mende.

Amidst the modest confines of their residence in Kaw Mende, life unfolded on the unadorned canvas of a single ground floor. To soften the hardness of this stark existence, Mr. Raymond, in his ever-resourceful manner, arranged a semblance of comfort. Beneath the beds, he laid down sturdy boards, layering them with a mat and a thick woolen cloth. It was a meager yet cherished attempt to imbue their dwelling with a touch of warmth. The much-anticipated move to the Mission House marked a momentous transition heralded by a whirlwind of excitement and anxiety. The very prospect of this change elicited palpable emotions, and Ann, in her delicate state, was not immune to their sway. Her senses were tinged with delirium, her thoughts awash with fervent concern for Mrs. Raymond, whom she perceived as fragile and in need of her care. She exerted herself beyond reason in this misdirected ardor, exposing her fragile constitution to the relentless African elements. The unyielding tropical climate conspired against her, seizing upon her vulnerability. A shivering cold settled into her lungs, leaving her with an enduring sense of breathlessness. The window, a meager barrier between their sanctuary and the sweltering exterior, remained perpetually ajar, an offering to the insatiable air.

Since their relocation to the Mission House, the specter of delirium shadowed Ann, refusing to relent. Vomiting, a constant companion of her suffering, relentlessly increased in frequency. Her appetite, once a source of vitality, dwindled into near oblivion. A humble gruel, concocted from ground rice and flour, was lovingly prepared by Mr. Raymond. Despite his best intentions, Ann's consumption dwindled precipitously. Over the span of three weeks, during which her ordeal culminated in a heart-wrenching conclusion, she could scarcely muster the strength to ingest a single quart of the nourishing gruel. In her altered reality, she perceived herself as sated, even overindulged, deluded by her infirmity. In the final days, as her body waged its relentless battle, she gave up all sustenance except water. Despite Mr. Raymond's unwavering efforts to persuade her to eat, she adamantly declined, professing fatigue or insisting she had already eaten. Ann was gripped by excessive purging, a relentless "flowing" that heralded an approaching change of unknown magnitude.

Mr. Raymond, a witness to her deteriorating state, was torn between hope and fear, knowing that a decisive shift was imminent yet unsure of the outcome.

On a fateful Wednesday morning, as the sun cast its hopeful rays upon the dimly lit room, Mr. Raymond ventured to inquire about Ann's condition. Tenderly, he approached her, a tremor of anticipation coursing through his being. The simple utterance of the word "better" was a rush of solace to his anxious heart. It resonated with the promise of recovery.

With a swiftness born of profound emotion, he set to prepare her a humble meal of gruel, his hands moving with a purpose fueled by love and hope. As he tenderly presented the nourishment he had prepared, she, weary yet resolute, demurred, claiming fatigue had temporarily stolen her appetite.

In these moments, her plaintive refrain was not pain but rather a persistent weariness, a tangible sign of her arduous journey.

Thursday morning dawned, a day filled with uncertainty, and Mr. Raymond hastened to her side, eager to gauge her condition again. Yet, this time, her response was a deafening silence, a haunting absence of words that foretold a growing insensibility. The shadow of impending loss loomed, but his heart, seasoned by countless similar vigils, harbored no immediate alarm.

As the clock continued its relentless march, approximately at the eighth hour, a subtle change in Ann's breathing stirred a whisper of concern within him. It was a shallow alteration, slight yet undeniable, that echoed the chorus of her prior complaints about the heavy burden of breathlessness. Mr. Raymond sat on the edge of her bed, his gaze fixed upon her, contemplating the possibilities before them.

In that sacred space, with her fragile hand in his own, he allowed himself to entertain the notion, however remote, that divine intervention might spare her. Mrs. Raymond, his beloved wife, had endured worse, and her spirit had persevered through Christ's power and God's mercy.

With unwavering faith, he departed briefly to convene his family for their daily prayer ritual for Ann's health, for even in the face of uncertainty, their faith remained steadfast.

Yet, as the words of scripture graced their ears, destiny, swift and unyielding, painted its final stroke. Returning to Ann's bedside, he beheld the onset of the inevitable, the ethereal dance of the death gasp. With a solemn call, he summoned his family to her side. With her hand cradled in his, Ann breathed her last breath, and her soul departed from her earthly vessel.

In the quietude of that solemn room, where the hushed breath of life mingled with the ethereal whisper of transition, Mr. Raymond grappled with the profound duality of his emotions. Grief, profound and relentless, threatened to overwhelm him like a tidal wave of sorrow, while the beacon of hope, radiant and unwavering, beckoned him to look toward the heavens. In this crucible of faith, his spirit wrestled, mirroring the struggles of a lifetime dedicated to the service of his Lord.

Ann's departure, her soul's passage into eternity, had left a void that reverberated in the depths of his heart. She had been not only a fellow missionary but also a beloved daughter, a kindred spirit whose presence illuminated their mission's darkest corners. He cherished her as he would his own flesh and blood, and now, just as the earthly bonds of affection had grown unbreakable, the cruel hand of fate had severed them. As he contemplated this, the ache of his grief seemed almost unbearable. Was it not enough that he had already traversed the harrowing path of losing a son, that tender bud of life taken from him prematurely? Now, with

Ann's passing, the anguish of losing a daughter, one he had nurtured and loved as if she were his own, weighed upon him like an insurmountable burden. In the stillness of his anguish, Mr. Raymond's thoughts circled like vultures over a wounded soul. Had God, in His divine wisdom, crafted a path that was too arduous, too fraught with sorrow? Were these trials too much to ask of him, the weight of two cherished lives resting heavily upon his shoulders? In his vulnerability, the questions resounded like a challenge to his faith, testing the foundation upon which he had built his life.

But in the darkest corners of despair, unwavering and resolute faith in God cast its radiant glow. The teachings of the Bible, a compass for his soul, guided him through the storm of doubt. He recalled the words of Jesus, the divine promise of eternal life, and the assurance that those who believed in Him would find solace beyond the confines of this earthly realm.

In the solitude of his mission quarters, Mr. Raymond wrestled with a profound crisis of faith, his heart heavy with the weight of two beloved souls lost to the relentless passage of time. As the leader of this missionary endeavor, he couldn't help but question the course of his journey, his role as a spiritual guide, and the sufficiency of his devotion.

The deaths of his infant son and Ann, who had become as dear to him as his own flesh and blood, cast a long shadow over his soul. Doubt, that insidious whisperer, taunted him.

Was he, in his frailty as a human, destined to carry such a heavy burden? Had God, in His infinite wisdom, designed this path as an unbearable test of his faith and resolve? The tears he shed in the silence of night bore witness to the depth of his despair.

Yet, in the midst of these doubt, he clung to the teachings of Christ. His fingers traced the words in his Bible, worn and marked with years of devout study. These verses like a lifeline, anchored him to the shores of faith.

"Do not let your hearts be troubled. You believe in God[a]; believe also in me. 2 My Father's house has many rooms; if that were not so, would I have told you that I am going there to prepare a place for you? 3 And if I go and prepare a place for you, I will come back and take you to be with me that you also may be where I am. 4 You know the way to the place where I am going."

– John 14:1-4

These words resonated within his soul, reminding him that beyond this temporal world lay an eternal abode, prepared with love by the Savior Himself. A place where souls found rest and peace, free from the trials of the earthly realm. With trembling hands, he turned to the Bible again, his heart seizing upon the apostle Paul's words:

"For to me, to live is Christ and to die is gain. ^{22} If I am to go on living in the body, this will mean fruitful labor for me. Yet what shall I choose? I do not know! ^{23} I am torn between the two: I desire to depart and be with Christ, which is better by far; ^{24} but it is more necessary for you that I remain in the body. ^{25} Convinced of this, I know that I will remain, and I will continue with all of you for your progress and joy in the faith, ^{26} so that through my being with you again your boasting in Christ Jesus will abound on account of me."

– Philippians 1:21-26

The very essence of his faith laid bare—life, a conduit for the glory of Christ, death, the gateway to eternal communion with the Savior. The delicate balance between these two desires, life and death, swayed within him like a pendulum. The longing to be reunited with his son and Ann, their souls dwelling in the presence of Christ, tugged at his very core. "I am torn between the two," he confessed. A profound longing for the eternal, a desire for reunion, and an unwavering conviction that his mission, his labor for Christ, remained incomplete. These verses, etched in the annals of his memory, came to life in his mind:

"^{12} Not that I have already obtained all this, or have already arrived at my goal, but I press on to take hold of that for which Christ Jesus took hold of me. ^{13} Brothers and sisters, I do not consider myself yet to have taken hold of it.

But one thing I do: Forgetting what is behind and straining toward what is ahead, [14] *I press on toward the goal to win the prize for which God has called me heavenward in Christ Jesus."*

– Philippians 3:12-14

The words carried a potent message. Though he had not yet reached the ultimate prize, the eternal dwelling promised to the faithful, he was compelled to keep pressing forward. To forget what lay behind, the heartache and loss, and to strain toward what lay ahead—the uncharted territory of God's divine purpose. The goal for which Christ had called him, heavenward, toward the eternal.

He contemplated these verses in his heart, each a beacon of divine guidance amidst the darkness of despair. His grief, profound and all-encompassing, began to shift, transforming into a vessel of purpose. The loss of his son and Ann, though an insurmountable burden, would not be in vain. Their lives, once intertwined with his own, had ignited a fervent desire within him to continue the labor of faith, to press on in his missionary work, and to be a beacon of Christ's love and salvation to those in need. His soul trembled on the precipice of revelation. The realization washed over him with a soothing grace—he had been chosen for this divine purpose.

The deaths of his son and Ann were not the culmination of God's plan but a part of the divine plan, threads of sorrow interwoven with threads of faith. In their memory, he would continue, propelled by the unwavering promise of Christ. The pain of loss left an indelible mark upon his heart, but it would serve as a testament to the resilience of faith, the enduring power of hope, and the unbreakable bond between man and his Creator.

In his grief-stricken solitude, he beseeched the Lord for strength, his prayers an earnest plea for guidance. The scriptures, a wellspring of solace, infused his spirit with renewed hope. He remembered the words:

> *"The Lord is close to the brokenhearted and saves those who are crushed in spirit."*
>
> **– Psalm 34:18**

In this sacred communion between man and his Creator, the weight of his despair began to lift, replaced by the gentle reassurance of divine grace. Mr. Raymond's grief, once an overwhelming storm, transformed into a steady undercurrent. The memories of Ann and his young son, once sources of sorrow, became vessels of hope, their souls now sheltered in the embrace of their heavenly Father. With each passing day, as he navigated the unpredictable terrain of loss, his faith grew stronger, an unwavering anchor in the storm. He envisioned Ann, clothed in robes of radiant light, standing in the presence of their Lord, her face aglow with the promise of eternal joy. The words that echoed in his heart were:

"He will wipe every tear from their eyes. There will be no more death or mourning or crying or pain, for the old order of things has passed away."

– **Revelation 21:4**

In this divine assurance, he found solace. The deep chasm of grief, which threatened to consume him, was bridged by the boundless promise of Jesus Christ. The teachings of the Bible, a beacon in the darkest hours, had illuminated his path once more. Mr. Raymond, though forever marked by loss, was emboldened by faith.

In his heart, the memory of Ann, the daughter he had lost, and his newborn son, whom he would one day embrace again, mingled with the profound conviction that their souls now resided in the eternal embrace of a loving God.

Chapter 8: Welcomed Home

In the heart of Sierra Leone's unforgiving landscape, where dense vegetation and untamed wilds embraced a modest mission outpost, a solitary figure stood against the relentless beat of the midday sun. William Raymond, a man of unyielding resolve yet burdened by grief, found himself grappling with the somber task of fashioning a final resting place for Ann L. Harnden.

The scene unfolded in a makeshift workshop, a humble corner of the mission compound where the absence of a nearby carpenter thrust Mr. Raymond into the role of coffin-maker. The sweltering air bore witness to the labor of love, a testimony to the confluence of practical necessity and emotional fortitude.

Mr. Raymond stood at the intersection of labor and lamentation. The air, thick with the humidity of an unforgiving day, bore witness to a scene both mundane and profoundly significant.

Children's laughter, a stark contrast to the weighty task at hand, reverberated through the mission compound. Their playful echoes, like ethereal notes of joy, intertwined with the melodic chirping of birds, creating music that underscored the dissonance of grief. In this paradoxical tableau, Mr. Raymond found himself the carpenter of solemn creations, crafting a vessel for farewell amidst the vibrancy of life. Mr. Raymond planned the construction of Ann's final abode. In the quiet recesses of the mission workshop, where the scent of sawdust lingered as a silent witness, he surveyed the tools of his trade. The task at hand, though born of obligation, took on a sacred hue.

To fashion a coffin was a necessity dictated by circumstance, but in the delicate dance of emotions, it became an unexpected communion with the departed.

As the children played and the birds sang, each note seemed to carve a gentle ache in Mr. Raymond's heart. The laughter, a reminder of life's persistent cadence, and the birdsong, an unwitting chorus of nature's indifference to human sorrow. Yet, at that moment where life and loss merged, the carpenter found an odd solace—the shared breath between creation and commemoration. The raw materials, once intended for more mundane purposes, now awaited transformation. The rhythmic sounds of his labor, the measured thud of hammer meeting nail, were punctuated by the occasional sigh—a release of emotions too profound for mere words.

In the act of constructing the coffin, his hands moved with a peculiar tenderness. Each stroke of the plane, each nail driven home, carried within it a silent conversation with Ann. It was a dialogue transcending the practicalities of carpentry—a communion of souls separated by the ethereal veil between life and death.

Mr. Raymond felt the paradox of emotions. The necessity of the task was an unyielding truth, yet, in its execution, it became a sacrament of remembrance. The seemingly mundane craftsmanship became a testimony to the profound intertwining of lives. The act of building Ann's final resting place, an endeavor fraught with sorrow, took on a sacred significance—a tribute offered in the language of wood and nails.

The beads of perspiration on his brow mirrored the toil of his heart. The unforgiving sun witnessed a soul grappling with the physical and metaphysical aspects of farewell. Each drop of sweat became an inadvertent libation—an offering poured out in the sacred act of remembrance.

The completion of the coffin, an undeniable reality, marked the culmination of this labor of love and sorrow. Stained black in solemn homage, it stood as an emblem of earthly goodbyes. Mr. Raymond, though weary from the physical exertion, found a peculiar solace in the tangible manifestation of his grief—the tangible expression of love for a departed soul. He stood in the shadow of the workshop. The completed coffin, a vessel for sacred memories, awaited its purpose.

The clearing near the mission house, where sorrow lingered like an unseen specter, revealed an unmarked plot of earth. Here, Ann's earthly remains would find their repose. Mr. Raymond and his wife had together decided upon the space. It was close to the grave of their own child, and since Ann was like a daughter to them, they decided that they would also like her to be with their little baby. Mr. Raymond looked at the site, his heart filling with emotion and the sense of loss threatening to overwhelm him. He felt as if he had lost two children in the span of a few months. Yet, he tried to focus on his work— the task at hand, making Ann's coffin with his own hands.

The craftsmanship, though born of necessity, transcended the utilitarian. Mr. Raymond, fueled by grit and determination, managed to create a coffin whose outward appearance defied the limitations of materials and circumstances. The stained exterior, a somber black, stood as a silent tribute to mourning, while the humble lining, not as refined as one might wish, spoke of the inherent constraints of mission life.

He was unsure of what to use for the shroud and for Ann's attire for the funeral and burial. He went to his wife for advice and comfort. Eliza Raymond, a fellow sojourner in the mission endeavor, offered a solution for Ann's attire in her final repose. Fine long nightgowns, once the property of Mrs. Tappan's departed daughter, found a new purpose as a makeshift shroud. They had been given to Mrs. Raymond, and now, she wished to give them to Ann.

A touching detail emerged in the form of a nightcap, a small yet significant choice that spoke to the tenderness with which Mr. Raymond approached his somber duties.

The nightcap, with its ample border, became an adornment for the departed, a quiet nod to the dignity inherent even in death. Mrs. Raymond suggested its use, and her husband thought it perfect for Ann. As he continued with the funeral preparations, he made his way to the river near the mission house.

There, he felt the oppressive burden of the somber time and sought the comfort of God. God sent him this in the form of his coxswain, Daddy George. Of this encounter, Mr. Raymond wrote in his letters: *Today the mission boat is on her way from Sierra Leone and is winding her way up the crooked river to the mission house. They are a mile or two below – they meet a canoe. "What news?" they inquire. One word is spoken and the boatman's arms are paralyzed. The oars lie motionless or but faintly perform their duty. What was that word which had such magic power? It was this, "Miss Ann is dead."*

I meet them at the wharf. All is still. Scarce a word is spoken. My soul is full. My coxswain "Daddy George" comes on shore. I take his hand in mine but cannot speak. He was the first one with whom I had met since Ann's death to whom I could open my soul and now my heart forbade me utterance. We walked in silence together to the house, I took him to the back door and pointed to the grave and think I said, "Yesterday", and turned away.

William Raymond, in a Letter to the Mendi Mission House, Dated August 10, 1844

Later, at the mission house, the air thick with both sorrow and the vibrant pulse of life, Mrs. Raymond stood in solemn preparation. Her heart, heavy with the weight of loss, found a unique communion with love in the final act of tenderness — the gentle care bestowed upon Ann's lifeless form.

Mrs. Raymond, her movements deliberate and tender, approached the solemn task with a heart both burdened and resolved. The pallor of grief painted her countenance as she beheld the lifeless vessel that once housed a spirit dear to her. Though unrelenting in its blaze, the afternoon sun cast a soft glow upon the scene as if nature paid homage to this sacred act. With measured grace, Mrs. Raymond began the tender ritual of cleansing, a ritual both mundane and profoundly significant.

Basin and cloth in hand, she approached Ann's still form, a daughter in death as much as in life. The water, cool against the warmth of the day, served as a gentle conduit between worlds — a final touch from a grieving 'mother' to her departed child. Mrs. Raymond, in this intimate act, allowed the waters of remembrance to flow, carrying away the earthly residue of a life now stilled. As she washed, each stroke of the cloth seemed a whispered prayer, a tender lamentation for moments now held only in memory. Her hands, once the source of comfort and guidance, became vessels of reverence, moving with a poignant cadence that belied the rawness of her grief.

The attire chosen for Ann's final repose, a garment that once adorned her in the vigor of life, now took on a sacred significance. Mrs. Raymond, her movements deliberate yet gentle, dressed the lifeless form in cloth and lace. The rustle of fabric seemed to echo the sentiments of a mother clothing her child in love for one last time.

The chosen attire, a vestige of a shared past, bore witness to a love that transcended the boundaries of life and death. The room, steeped in the sacred fragrance of nostalgia, became a sanctuary for this intimate communion between the living and the departed.

While Mrs. Raymond prepared Ann's body for its final journey, her movements carried the weight of farewell. Outside, under the unyielding gaze of the Sierra Leone's sun, Mr. Raymond undertook his own preparations. He moved with a solemn purpose. The King, the other missionaries, and the community at large had to be informed of the impending farewell.

In measured steps, Mr. Raymond traversed the mission compound, a bearer of both tidings and burdens. His voice, a steady cadence amidst the quietude, relayed the news of the impending funeral. The king, a dignitary in his own right, received the message with a nod of understanding — a shared acknowledgment of the universality of grief. The other missionaries, bound by a shared mission and now a shared sorrow, lent their support in solemn agreement. Words were unnecessary in this communion of grief, for the weight of loss was a universally understood language.

As the announcement resonated through the community, the solemn hum of acknowledgment permeated the air. The people prepared to bear witness to a farewell that transcended cultural boundaries. The mission house awaited the final act of parting. The aroma of freshly hewn wood mingled with the sacred fragrance of remembrance, creating an atmosphere where earthly farewells met the ethereal. In this convergence of preparation, within the quiet spaces where love and loss intertwined, the Raymonds navigated the delicate dance between duty and devotion.

Mrs. Raymond, a sentinel of tender rituals, adorned Ann in the attire of love's last embrace, while Mr. Raymond, the bearer of solemn tidings, orchestrated the communal response to a departure that echoed beyond the mission compound. The sacred act of bidding farewell to Ann unfolded within the walls of the mission house. The air, heavy with the fragrance of memory and the anticipation of divine presence, cradled the assembled mourners in a cocoon of shared grief.

In the hushed sanctum of sorrow, Mr. Raymond, now clad in the vestments of stewardship, guided the congregation through the sacred liturgy of loss. The flickering candles cast a warm glow upon the bowed heads and tear-stained faces, a reminder that even in the depths of grief, a divine light permeated the darkness. The pages of the Bible rustled, and the timeless verses of comfort resonated through the chamber. Amidst the sea of mourners, Mrs. Raymond, her countenance a canvas of restrained sorrow, stood as a beacon of faith. The chosen Scriptures, each word a balm for the wounded soul, echoed through the halls, weaving a narrative transcending the temporal.

The hymns, born from the collective voices of those who sought solace in shared melodies, soared into the heavens. The harmonies, fragile yet resolute, resonated through the hearts of the mourners. In the lyrics, the promise of eternal peace, mingled with the ache of earthly separation, presented both hope and lament.

Fervent and heartfelt prayers rose like incense, ascending to the divine realms. Mr. Raymond, his voice a steady conduit between the earthly and the ethereal, invoked the mercy of the Almighty. The mourners, their souls laid bare before the Creator, found solace in the communion of shared petitions. The journey to the graveside commenced as the final notes of a hymn lingered in the air. The mission compound, now a sacred threshold, bore witness to the convergence of earthly sorrow and Godly grace. The rays of the setting sun, a celestial benediction, cast a golden hue upon the gathered mourners, elevating the farewell from mere ritual to sacred sacrament.

As the congregation approached the graveside, a profound stillness enveloped the scene. The freshly turned earth cradled the awaiting vessel.

Mr. and Mrs. Raymond gathered the faithful and began the farewell prayers for Ann.

As the mourners bowed their heads in collective supplication, Mr. Raymond, a shepherd of souls, raised his voice in a prayer that resonated with hope.

"Almighty Father, we stand before You, hearts laid bare in the crucible of grief. In this moment of parting, grant us the solace that flows from Your eternal promises. We commend our beloved Ann into Your loving embrace, knowing that Your mercy transcends the boundaries of time and space." Mrs. Raymond led the mourners in songs that spoke of heavenly reunion.

"Oh, the bliss of that glorious day, when with the ransomed in glory, her joyous song will echo through the halls of eternity. Let our voices rise, not in despair, but in a resounding affirmation of the eternal life she now enjoys in Your heavenly kingdom."

The Scriptures, a reservoir of divine wisdom and solace, unfolded through Mr. Raymond's words. "Brothers and sisters, let us turn to the sacred pages that remind us of the promises that await the faithful. In John 14, our Lord and Savior assures us, *'Do not let your hearts be troubled. Believe in God; believe also in me. In my Father's house are many rooms... I go to prepare a place for you.'* Let this truth be our anchor in the storm of grief—Ann now dwells in the rooms prepared by the hands of our Savior."

Mr. Raymond, with unwavering conviction, proclaimed the Christian hope.

"In Philippians, we find the Apostle Paul's resounding declaration: *'For to me, to live is Christ and to die is gain.'* Ann has crossed the threshold of earthly existence, and her gain is the eternal communion with Christ. Though tears may blur our vision, let the eyes of faith perceive the radiant glory awaiting her." Mrs. Raymond, standing amidst the congregation, offered her heartfelt entreaties. *"Heavenly Father, in this moment of earthly parting, grant us the strength to release Ann into Your divine care. As we lower her earthly vessel into the waiting embrace of the earth, may our spirits soar with the assurance that she now dwells in the celestial realms, free from pain and sorrow."*

The benediction, a sacred seal upon the gathered assembly, echoed through the mission house. *"May the peace that surpasses all understanding guard your hearts and minds in Christ Jesus. As we carry the memory of Ann in our earthly pilgrimage, let us walk with the unwavering hope that, one day, we shall be reunited in the glorious presence of our Lord."*

The committal, a sacred dialogue between the earthly and the divine, unfolded. Mr. Raymond, his gaze fixed on the heavens, uttered words that transcended the boundaries of mortal understanding. The gathered mourners, their hearts a chorus of shared lament, listened to the echo of promises that stretched beyond the veil. The mourners, their steps heavy with the weight of earthly parting, left the graveside with a shared prayer on their lips—a prayer that echoed the eternal refrain of Christian hope. In the aftermath of the sacred liturgy, as the shadows deepened and the stars emerged, the mission house stood as a sanctuary of solace.

The Raymonds, with hearts both heavy and uplifted, found solace in the promise that the tears shed in earthly farewells watered the gardens of heavenly reunion. It was in the introspection following the funeral that the profound truth of Raymond's emotional armor unfolded.

The seeming detachment maintained during the laborious tasks was not indifference but a mercy of providence. It was a preservation mechanism, a grace bestowed by God, shielding him from the full weight of his loss. The acknowledgment of this defense mechanism lent a poignant depth to the narrative, revealing the delicate balance between grief and the need for functional action.

The exhaustion, both physical and emotional, lingered like a shadow. The hard work and the excruciating reality of crafting Ann's final abode exacted a toll on Raymond. From it was a slow recovery, the gradual mending of a soul burdened by sorrow and labor.

On the day of Ann's funeral, Mr. Raymond was shattered. He poured out his heart on a scrap of paper and laid himself bare, etching his feelings and grief into his words. The Letter read:

Mendi Mission House

August 9, 1844

And is it so? Must I, can I believe it? Is it true? It is must be though my mind cannot realize it. It is true. I sat upon her bedside and held her hand in mine and watched her flickering breath to the last. These hands of mine closed her eyes in death. These same hands put upon her the robe of death. They made for her the narrow house and helped put her into it. I have knelt by the side of her grave and heard that hollow sound which came from thence. It is true Ann is dead. I look into her room – it is desolate. A death like silence reigns through the house. There seems something wanting. Our family seems like a watch that has lost one of its principal wheels.

Last night I threw my wearied body upon my bed to rest. Sleep I would not. Hark! I thought I heard that sweet voice softly say "Maria" as it used to speak it. I started up in my bed. But ah! How mistaken true those lips were there but they were locked in death. (Maria was particularly her girl. She always stayed in her room when I was not there and slept there when I did not.)

As I now sit to write I cast my eyes out of the door and behold a new made heap of earth. It was not there this morning. Beneath that heap of earth this hat belongs to earth of the one we loved – but stop.

Why am I so groveling? Why am I diving down to the bottom of the grave when our sister is not there? Why not rather follow that cloud of angels which bore her ransomed spirit to the mansion prepared for it? Lord gives me faith and I will try. Let us step back to yester morn. That was a silent solemn hour. Tears were she then. When shall I forget it? "Let my right hand forget her cunning and my tongue cleave to the roof of my mouth, in that day death was there, but he had no sting. Look! Who are these?

"Bright angels have from glory come

They're round her bed, They're in her room

They wait to waft her spirit home"

With me they watch the fleeting breath. It is done. The struggling spirit is free. It has escaped from death's embrace and mounts on angel's wings and is borne upward away. Where I sat watching to see if there was to be still another gasp, she had already reached those pearly gates – already had entered those golden streets. Hark! Do you hear? Heaven's hallelujahs receive a new impulse.

They grow higher and higher still, another ransomed soul safe in glory. Bring hither the crown of gold, the white robe and the golden harp. Glory, honor, praise and power be unto the Lamb forever. Hallelujah, Amen.

She is now crowned a king, priest unto her God forever. Me thinks I see her now. She approaches the throne and casts her crown at the feet of Him who sits upon it. Hark! Do you hear those sweet, those heavenly – those glorious strains which flow from off that harp? Did you think our "Little" sister Ann could ever make such music – How sweet- how ravishing. My own soul begins to catch the flame.

> *"I want, oh I want to be there*
>
> *I want to be one of your choir*
>
> *And turn my own harp to His praise."*

William Raymond

Chapter 9: Quieted Shoes

In the sanctum of William Raymond's study, the air was laden with the fragrance of aging wood and ink and the weight of grief, a palpable presence that seemed to ripple through the flickering candlelight. Mr. Raymond, a man of both earthly duties and Godly convictions, stood at the precipice of parchment and quill, contemplating the sacred act before him.

The sun outside, in its relentless course, cast an unyielding glow, and beyond the windows, the vibrant hues of tropical flora seemed oblivious to the somber task within. The distant laughter of playing children, the gentle rustling of leaves, and the melodic cadence of birdsong formed an unwitting backdrop to the sacred undertaking. Yet, for Mr. Raymond, their joyous existence only accentuated the solemnity of his penance—a tribute to a departed soul and an offering to God.

As the quill touched the ink, it seemed to draw from the well not merely the black liquid but the essence of sorrow that dwelled within the recesses of a grieving heart. The first strokes upon the parchment were tentative as if navigating a path through the thicket of emotions that had taken residence within him. The inkwells, filled with solemn contents, became vessels of shared lamentation and sacred reminiscence. With each scribbled word, Mr. Raymond felt the stirring of memories—the crafting of the coffin beneath the relentless sun, the trembling hands as he prepared Ann for her final rest, and the communal prayers uttered in the sacred space of the mission house. A few days had passed since her funeral, but the weight of the grief was still heavy and fresh. The ink seemed to absorb the narrative of earthly farewells and the essence of a promise that lay beyond.

In the act of writing, his heart wrestled with the responsibility he felt toward Ann's family. Did Ann's mother, in a distant land, feel the impact of her daughter's departing from this world and into the next? The Bible, a well-worn companion, lay open beside him—a source of solace and guidance. Verses of comfort, passages of hope, and promises of eternal reunion provided both anchor and sail as he navigated the currents of grief. Yet, amidst the solemnity, there was a subtle grace—a realization that, in crafting this epistle, he drew closer to the departed one. Detailing Ann's journey became an offering, a channel through which earthly sorrow could be transmuted into a sacred narrative of hope. The parchment, pristine and eager, lay before him. He dipped the quill in ink, and the writing began, each stroke a prayer, each sentence a vessel carrying the weight of an earthly farewell. He wrote:

Mendi Mission House, Little Boom River

Sherbro, West Africa

August 25th, 1844

My Dear Sister Harnden,

I have been led to think much of you of late and now sit down to write you. Where to begin I know not. It is painful to be the bearer of unpleasant news but especially so when we ourselves are in the affliction. To come to it at once, that beloved daughter of yours whom you so freely devoted to God, He has taken to Himself.

It is true though I can hardly make myself believe it. Ann is dead. She died about 9 o'clock on Thursday morning August 8th. He detailed the nature of Ann's illness to her mother so that she would be able to know that they had done all they could for her beloved daughter.

Ann was always happy and contented here. The last thing that I remember of hearing her say about her soul before she became delirious was that she felt the witness in her soul that God had sent her here from the time we left New York till she became delirious there was a steady growth in grace and in the knowledge of the Gospel.

There seemed to be more and more of a sinking into Jesus. In her death you have suffered with a great loss but it does not seem to me that mine is less. She was your child. So she was mine. You gave her to me and told me to be a father to her.

Whether I was or not is not for me to say but she was a child to me. I always called her my child when I spoke to her. By her death I am left alone. My Father saw fit to deprive my dear wife of her reason so that I could not go to her to tell my trials. I could then go to Ann and find a sympathizing heart. Now I am alone. No one to whom I can unbosom my bursting heart. When Ann was with us well enough to be about the house, she was mistress of the family and everything was in order. Now I have to hire a house keeper in addition to all my other cares. My wife and Ann were like two sisters.

Their souls were knit together. I sometime feared we loved her too much. God has separated us and taken her Himself and my soul unbosomer says Amen. Our Father would not have taken if he had not need of her.

I will send you her chest of clothes by the first opportunity after the dry season commences. I cut off all her back hair which I will send in the chest. I am unable to give as many particulars as I wish in this small sheet.

I intend to write to Mary and to Dr. Martyn. You may find things in their letters which I cannot put in here. Ann is gone we feel your loss but our loss is her eternal gain.

Your brother in affliction,

Wm Raymond

Upon completing the letter, Mr. Raymond sealed the parchment, a sacred vessel carrying the echoes of a soul's journey.

As he prepared it for dispatch, his gaze turned to the heavens, seeking assurance in the promise that the God of all comfort would cradle both the words and the grieving hearts in His infinite love.

The ink-stained quill lay still, having etched the earthly narrative onto the parchment, and now, the man of God turned his gaze toward the living scriptures that adorned the pages of the Bible beside him.

His eyes fell upon the verses he had pondered countless times—the tried and tested words that had been a steadfast companion through the storms of life. John 14:1-4 spoke of a heavenly dwelling prepared by the Savior, a mansion with room enough for weary souls to find solace.

"Do not let your hearts be troubled. You believe in God; believe also in me. My Father's house has many rooms; if that were not so, would I have told you that I am going there to prepare a place for you? And if I go and prepare a place for you, I will come back and take you to be with me that you also may be where I am. You know the way to the place where I am going."

– John 14:1-4

As the words resonated in his mind, he felt a profound connection between this promise and the eternal home Ann had embraced. Philippians 1:21-26, with its poignant duality of living for Christ and gaining in death, echoed through the chambers of his contemplation.

Not that I have already obtained all this, or have already arrived at my goal, but I press on to take hold of that for which Christ Jesus took hold of me. Brothers and sisters, I do not consider myself yet to have taken hold of it. But one thing I do: Forgetting what is behind and straining toward what is ahead, I press on toward the goal to win the prize for which God has called me heavenward in Christ Jesus.

– Philippians 1:21-26

Was this not the crux of their missionary journey? To live was Christ, and for Ann, to die was an ascent into the very presence of the One they served. In Philippians 3:12-14, he found a resolute call to press on, to forget what was behind, and to strain toward the heavenly goal. The losses, the trials, and the earthly farewells were but mile-markers on the path to eternal peace. In the solitude of his study, Mr. Raymond found a renewed vigor to press on, to fulfill the mission that both transcended and was grounded in the temporal.

Yet, the verses were not merely inscriptions on parchment; they were living, breathing truths that intersected with the fabric of his own existence. The loss of a son and now a daughter—each a poignant echo of the brevity of earthly sojourn. As he pondered the pages, William grappled not only with the theology of solace but with the practicality of a life that bore witness to these truths. In the dim glow of the candlelight, he began to see the intertwining of the sacred and the earthly, the ethereal promises finding resonance in the mundane occurrences of missionary toil. Each footstep on the path to the graveside, every word uttered in communal prayer, and the crafting of a makeshift coffin—all became sacraments, tangible expressions of an unwavering faith. A profound stillness descended upon the room, punctuated only by the rustling of leaves outside and the distant sounds of life in the village. The man of God, a shepherd tending to a flock on both sides of eternity, found solace in the harmonies of the scriptures. They were not mere verses; they were living waters that quenched the thirst of a soul journeying through the arid landscapes of earthly toil.

As the night wore on, Mr. Raymond, missionary and pastor, emerged from the sanctum of contemplation, his spirit renewed by the promises that transcended the temporal. The letter, though sealed and destined for distant lands, was not merely a message of mourning but a testament to the hope that flowed from the Word of God. The ink-stained quill had not only etched narratives of parting but had inscribed upon the parchment the resolute proclamation that, in Christ, even farewells were but preludes to reunions in heaven. He placed the sealed letter atop a small wooden crate that was to become a repository of cherished remnants. The crate was to be filled with Ann's belongings and would be sent to her mother. One memento held a profound place among Ann's earthly remnants; it was the only thing already inside the crate —the tight bow of ebony strands, remnants of her once-vibrant black hair.

It had been a moment of poignant intimacy when Mr. Raymond, a surrogate father to Ann, undertook the solemn task of severing those locks from her lifeless form. The gleaming scissors whispered through the still air, their silver blades biting through the tendrils that once framed her face. With each cut, the strands fell, silent witnesses to a farewell that transcended the mortal realm. A scrap of fabric, gifted by a Mende child and lovingly held by Ann, served as the humble binding for this sacred relic. Mr. Raymond gave those locks to his wife, along with the cloth.

As Mrs. Raymond had tied the bow to secure the hair, her hands moved with a grace that belied the heaviness in her heart. She, too, felt the weight of the moment, the bittersweet act of preserving a piece of the departed.

For Mr. Raymond, it had been an act of love and an embodiment of the finality of the earthly journey. He had paced the hair into a box and laid it inside her crate. He opened the crate to take out the box of Ann's hair. With trembling hands, he opened it. As he looked upon the bow concealed in the box, memories cascaded like shadows. The laughter that once danced around her, the earnest questions she posed, and the quiet moments of shared prayer—all found a semblance of presence in that tiny repository. He placed the box and the letter into the crate, a tear escaping his eye.

Now, as the sealed letter rested atop the box, a charge to convey not only words but also the tangible fragments of life extinguished too soon, Mr. Raymond sought his wife. They convened in the dimly lit study, the weight of the task ahead casting a subdued hush upon their conversation. Gently, he broached the subject of which belongings to send—a dialogue steeped in practicality and emotion. They made their way to Ann's room together. Mr. Raymond took the crate with him, holding onto it as if it housed his own child.

The small room became a haven for reminiscence as they sifted through Ann's belongings. Each item, a vessel of memory, bore witness to the intersection of two worlds—the Mende village and a Massachusetts home.

The process became a ritual of sorts. A worn Bible, its pages echoing with her annotations, sparked discussions of shared devotion and spiritual milestones. A threadbare quilt, stitched together from familiar and foreign cloths, spoke of nights warmed by a shared humanity beneath the African skies.

But it was the bow of hair, nestled within the box, that anchored their contemplations. Mr. Raymond's voice wavered as he recalled the tender act of severance, and his wife, eyes glistening, spoke of the care with which she had bound it—a ribbon of grief and remembrance. As they pondered each article, the prospect of dispatching these fragments of Ann's world across the vast expanse of ocean weighed heavily. The crate, intended as a vessel of closure, was to become a vessel of transit, charged with ferrying not only possessions but the echoes of life back to a mother yearning for connection. Surrounded by the artifacts of a shared journey, they wrestled with the paradox of this farewell. The belongings, so lovingly chosen, were to embark on a pilgrimage from the sunlit shores of Sierra Leone to the distant harbor of Massachusetts. The journey would be arduous and fraught with the uncertainty of the sea.

The task of dispatching these remnants to a grieving mother was not merely logistical; it was a gesture showing the expansiveness of love, which, like the ceaseless waves that spanned oceans, defied the constraints of distance and time.

Mr. Raymond retreated to the solace of his bedroom, weary from the day's emotional toil. Meanwhile, Mrs. Raymond, fueled by a blend of devotion and maternal tenderness, remained in the dim glow of Ann's room, continuing with the task.

Her nimble fingers traversed the belongings that bore the imprint of Ann's vibrant presence. Each item, a relic of shared moments and spiritual journeys, became a vessel of connection between two worlds. As Mrs. Raymond traversed the landscape of Ann's remnants, the atmosphere hummed with a bittersweet melody—a sonnet of memory, love, and the profound embrace of faith. An unfinished letter lay atop the worn wooden desk. Mrs. Raymond, her gaze softened by a maternal understanding, unfolded the creased pages. Ann's words, suspended in the dance of ink, bridged by heaven and earth. Reading it, Mrs. Raymond felt a heavenly connection—a dialogue with a soul traversing the realms of existence.

The knitting work, left in a state of perpetual incompletion, spoke of the interrupted rhythm of daily life. The intricate patterns whispered tales of shared afternoons and the joy found in the gentle hum of needles.

Dresses, meticulously sewn by Ann's hands, became more than fabric and stitches. They were garments of love—each fold, each seam, a testimony to the artistry of devotion. As Mrs. Raymond held them, the rustle of fabric echoed with shared laughter and the whispered secrets of shared sisterhood. Ann's shoes, once witnesses to dances in the moonlit courtyard, now rested in silent repose. Mrs. Raymond cradled them, feeling the imprint of a departed loved one in the worn soles.

The essence of those shoes, a fusion of earthly wanderings and heavenly aspirations, became a metaphor for the journey of faith—the footsteps of a missionary navigating the crossroads of devotion and destiny.

The hairbrush, adorned with strands that once framed Ann's countenance, held the tactile echo of a touch. Mrs. Raymond, brushing her fingers over the now-still bristles, felt the intangible connection—a maternal gesture. The book about the Mende people, Ann's curiosity and cultural exploration bound in pages, became a testament to a missionary's heart. Mrs. Raymond, thumbing through the chapters, sensed Ann's unquenchable thirst for understanding—a spiritual sojourner navigating the intricate landscapes of faith and cultural exchange. The Bible, adorned with annotations and echoes of Ann's spiritual sojourns, lay open before her. The notes, penned with an earnest hand, bore witness to a faith journey as Ann had written in it only after departing for Mende. Mrs. Raymond traced the verses, her fingers following the sacred lines—a silent conversation with a departed soul whose faith had transcended the earthly realm. A small stack of prayers and Bible verses, handwritten and adorned with delicate illustrations, lay on the bedside table. Each piece of parchment, a brushstroke in the portrait of Ann's connection with the divine, radiated the warmth of faith.

Finally, Mrs. Raymond added into the chest the Robin Broach that Ann had been given at the beginning of her journey and mission. The broach was continually pinned to her dress, a reminder of the people who Ann was working for in God and a reminder that she was touching the lives of so many.

The pin had made Ann feel appreciated and loved. She had worn it as a symbol of solidarity with her Christian brethren. Mrs. Raymond knew about how significant the broach was for Ann. The beautiful piece had been placed on her dress for the funeral but before she was buried, Mrs. Raymond retrieved the pin. Now, she took it out of her pocket and placed it in the chest for Ann's mother to receive.

She hoped that the significance of the pin would be understood and that it could become a cherished heirloom in the family. To make this possible, Mrs. Raymona also added in a note, telling Mrs. Harnden all about the pin. Mrs. Raymond entered a sacred dialogue with these belongings as she touched each one and was flooded with memories and emotions. She shared a whispered prayer for the departed and a hymn of gratitude for the shared moments of spiritual exploration.

Amidst these relics, she communed with the divine—a silent conversation with the Almighty. The room, suffused with a spiritual resonance, became a sacred space where earthly remnants metamorphosed into vessels of eternal connection. In the memories of Ann's belongings, she glimpsed the fingerprints of God—a divine choreography of faith.

As the night advanced, Mrs. Raymond remained enveloped in the communion of remembrance. Each item, cradled in her hands, whispered tales of a life well-lived and a faith journey that transcended the earthly horizon.

Chapter 10: Seeds Sown

In the stillness of the mission house, one year after Ann's untimely departure, William Raymond, guided by profound faith, found solace in the divine orchestration of God's will.

As he stood before the threshold of anniversaries, he rejoiced not in the absence of pain but in the assurance that Ann, nestled in the loving arms of her God, had transcended the clutches of earthly trials and the snares of Satan.

The mission, a living testament to the indomitable spirit of Christian devotion, continued to unfurl its sacred purpose on the fertile soil of Sierra Leone. In the wake of Ann's passing, the flame of missionary zeal burned with an unwavering brightness.

The communal spirit, once intertwined with Ann's vivacity, had transformed into a resilient force—an embodiment of the divine charge to persist in the face of adversity.

Ann's earthly departure had cast a shadow, but in the corridors of the mission, the echoes of her legacy resonated.

The impact of her life, much like ripples on a tranquil pond, had far-reaching consequences. The Mende people, touched by her compassion and inspired by her resilience, found solace in the continuation of the mission. Ann's teachings, her gentle demeanor, and her unwavering commitment to the Christian cause became embedded in the fabric of the missionary endeavor.

About Ann, Mr. Raymond wrote in a letter:

"One thing that made Ann peculiarly dear to us was this. When she first came with us, we found her but a child in the Gospel. She had consecrated her all, yet she was but a child. Things we had learned years before she knew nothing about. But we found in her a teachable spirit and she learnt in months what it had taken us years to learn. If ever I felt happy in my life it was in expounding, it unto her the way of God more perfectly. Often would she bring questions of duty, etc. to me. Never in my life did I see such progress made by any individual as was made by her the short time she was with us.

I thought God was preparing her for eminent usefulness in this field, but he was preparing her for himself and she is now doubtless employed though in another sphere yet perhaps in the same field.

I do not think our work is done when we leave the body. True our bodily labors end but still our spirits are engaged I think in the same great work of salvation. And this morning while our hearts are bleeding on account of our loss, Ann perhaps is laboring with ten times the efficiency she would be if she were with us. Then my sister while our hearts are laid open to their very core and they are bleeding at every pore, let us rejoice in God who doeth all things well. Let us rejoice in the will of our Father who does not willingly afflict his children but makes everything work together for their good."

The mission, a collective endeavor fueled by the synergy of devoted souls, found motivation in the memory of Ann. In the face of challenges and tribulations, her life became a beacon—a testament to the enduring power of faith. The missionaries, galvanized by the spirit of their departed sister, moved forward with a renewed sense of purpose. Each step, guided by the teachings of Christ, became a pilgrimage—a sacred sojourn toward a vision of spiritual enlightenment.

The impact of Ann's passing, far from diminishing the mission, served as a catalyst for spiritual fortitude. The collective grief, rather than stifling the flame, fueled an unwavering commitment to the cause. The Mende people, resilient witnesses to the ebb and flow of missionary endeavors, continued to be touched by the transformative power of Christ's love.

The mission emerged as a living parable—a narrative of redemption, resilience, and unwavering devotion. The missionaries found a wellspring of strength in the communion of shared labor, prayers, and divine purpose. Ann's memory, far from being relegated to the recesses of the past, became an abiding presence—an invisible hand guiding the missionary enterprise toward the heavenly realms. Within the mission's life, Ann's passing became not a lamentable failure but a resounding victory. William Raymond, standing at the nexus of earthly endeavors and divine purpose, perceived her departure not as an absence but as a call to emulate her selfless commitment. Her willingness to give everything to the cause became a clarion call to those who remained—to offer their all in the pursuit of a mission imbued with the fervor of divine purpose.

The void left by Ann's physical absence resonated most profoundly in the hearts of the children of Mende. Once the recipients of her tender care, the little ones felt the absence keenly. Yet, undeterred by the challenge, the mission worked ardently to fill the void with renewed inspiration and steadfast dedication. Ann's memory, a guiding light, infused the mission with an enduring commitment to the children.

The children, once touched by Ann's affectionate presence, continued to be the heartbeat of the endeavor. They worked even harder in their studies and attended the events of the mission regularly. Their laughter, like a hymn of innocence, intermingled with the earnest prayers rising from the mission house. Ann's absence, though palpable, transformed into an indomitable spirit—an invisible force that guided the missionaries in their quest to provide spiritual nourishment to the young souls. The mission sustained the intensity of engagement with the children. Language barriers, though formidable, crumbled under the collective will to learn and communicate. Their commitment to understanding and adopting the nuances of the local dialect became a testament to the universality of Christian love—a language that transcends the barriers of speech and resonates in the chambers of the heart. The spirit of Ann inspired the missionaries to construct a new narrative, and the mission continued to thrive as a haven for the young minds eager to embrace the teachings of Christ.

The resonance of the Gospel message echoed through Sierra Leone. The people, drawn by the unwavering dedication of the missionaries, slowly but surely became connected to the divine narrative. The seeds of faith, sown by Ann and nurtured by those who followed in her footsteps, sprouted into a garden of spiritual awakening. The mission, guided by the principles of Christian love and compassion, became a conduit for the transformative power of the gospel—a beacon that attracted those seeking solace in the arms of divine grace.

As the mission house stood steadfast against the passage of time, the missionaries found renewed purpose in their collective endeavor. The absence of one became the rallying cry for many, and in the sacred space of the mission, the legacy of Ann endured. The victory of sacrificial love and unwavering commitment in the pursuit of God's divine purpose was the force that propelled the mission forward.

The missionary efforts led by William Raymond unfolded as a compassionate melding of education, spiritual guidance, and ethical teachings. The mission, borne out of a commitment to serve both the temporal and spiritual needs of the people, became a beacon of hope and transformation. At the heart of the mission's endeavors lay the pursuit of education—an essential tool for empowerment and upliftment. In the shadows of towering trees, children gathered beneath makeshift classrooms, their eyes alight with the curiosity of young minds hungry for knowledge. The missionaries, undeterred by challenges, strived to provide a sanctuary of learning where literacy and numeracy could flourish.

The curriculum extended beyond the confines of conventional textbooks. Lessons became a blend of academic wisdom and practical life skills. The rustling leaves bore witness to classes where children deciphered the written word and learned the art of sustenance—cultivating crops and understanding the symbiotic dance between earth and seed. Sunday, a sacred day on the missionary calendar, unfurled as a beacon of spiritual enlightenment. The makeshift church, adorned with the vibrant hues of native blossoms, echoed with hymns of faith and sermons that sought to weave the teachings of the Gospel into the fabric of everyday existence. Families, clad in their best attire, gathered to partake in the communion of souls.

The guidance offered by the missionaries transcended the spiritual realm. William Raymond, assuming roles beyond that of a religious leader, became a shepherd guiding his flock through the complexities of life. Whether counseling on matters of family, resolving disputes, or offering solace in times of grief, the mission assumed the mantle of a steadfast ally in the lives of the people.

Ethics and character-building became integral facets of the mission's impact. Beneath the overarching canopy of trees, stories from the Bible transformed into ethical guidelines that illuminated the path of righteousness.

The missionaries embodied the principles they sought to instill—becoming living parables of compassion, humility, and integrity. The mission, like a bountiful garden, tended with care, bore the fruit of transformation. Families once bound by the shackles of ignorance found themselves equipped with the tools of knowledge, breaking free from the cyclical chains of poverty. The seeds of faith sprouted into a community bound by a shared spiritual journey. Amidst the challenges posed by the tropical terrain and the intricate dance of cultural nuances, the missionaries remained undeterred. The impact of their efforts resonated in the stories of lives changed—of children educated, families united, and souls finding solace in the embrace of divine love.

The missionaries found a profound truth—the mission, beyond the temporal realm, was an eternal testament to the resilience of Christian devotion. In the celestial symphony that echoed through the mission, Ann's song, though silenced in the earthly realm, continued to resonate with them as an anthem of faith, love, and the enduring legacy of a Christian mission that persevered even in the face of earthly farewells. They found an unassailable strength in their reliance on God. The words of the Apostle Paul, echoing through the ages, became the steadfast mantra that fortified their resolve: *"I can do all things through Jesus Christ who strengthens me."* It was not merely a biblical verse; it became the anthem of their daily endeavors, a source of unwavering strength drawn from the wellspring of divine grace.

As the missionaries weathered the seasons of grief and adaptation, they found solace in the understanding that Ann's passing was not the end of their collective mission. Instead, it marked a poignant punctuation—an exclamation point that compelled them to redouble their efforts to serve the higher calling. The mission emerged as a living testament to the resilience of faith in the face of earthly trials.

The king, a witness to the enduring commitment of the missionaries, eventually approached them with a request. After a year marked by both tribulations and triumphs, he asked them to leave. He was a descendant of John Tucker who in 1665, as an agent in the service of the Gambia Adventurers, left England and went to Sierra Leone alongside Zachary Rogers. Upon arriving in Sherbro Country, John Tucker and Zachary Rogers took the daughters of a Sherbro chief as their wives as was customary in order to gain trading rights in the region.

The Tuckers would become one of the most influential and prominent Sherbro families during the 17th and 18th centuries, and were able to expand their powerful chiefdom into other territories. Now in the mid-19th century, Chief Harry Tucker is faced with deciding between the roots of his own heritage and following the call of Christ on his life. Not proud of that heritage and all that came with it he struggled with letting go. He felt as though he was losing his authority as Mr. Raymond's popularity grew. These people were his people, and he had once been their confidant and counselor. He felt his influence waning. The time had come to once again take the role of their earthly king. The very soil they had trodden upon, the air that had borne witness to their prayers and hymns, whispered the inevitability of change. It was a bittersweet moment—a culmination of a chapter enriched by Ann's influence and a prelude to new territories awaiting the seeds of Christian love.

As the missionaries prepared to depart, William Raymond found himself immersed in reflections on the year that had passed. The echo of Ann's laughter, the resonance of her fervent prayers, lingered in the corridors of the mission house. Amidst the melancholy, a profound realization settled in his heart. He pondered over the transient nature of earthly plans, recognizing the futility of mapping out the journey of faith with predetermined precision. Never again would he plan for God, realizing that the divine narrative unfolded in ways beyond human comprehension. Ann's passing, though a heart-rending chapter, became a catalyst for a deeper surrender to the will of God. In the crucible of missionary life, he learned the profound truth that transcended the boundaries of his grief—the assurance that God's plan, though mysterious, unfolded with greater purpose and meaning. With a heavy heart, yet fortified by the enduring strength of faith, the missionaries bid farewell to the mission that had been their sanctuary and crucible for a while. The lessons learned, the lives touched, and the indomitable spirit of Ann's legacy accompanied them as they embarked on a new phase of their journey—a journey guided by the unwavering belief that they could do all things through Jesus Christ, who strengthened them.

In the quietness of Sierra Leone, where the tropical air hung heavy with the fragrance of exotic blooms and the symphony of vibrant birdsong echoed through the verdant landscape, William Raymond found himself contemplating a poignant farewell. The time had come to embark on a journey beyond the confines of the mission—a journey that beckoned him toward a meeting with Ann's mother, a soul intricately connected to the intricate tapestry of his mission and the story of Ann's profound sacrifice. For a long time, the written word had bridged the physical distance between William and Ann's mother. Letters, penned with ink that bore the weight of shared grief and unwavering faith, traversed the vast expanse of the Atlantic, forming a lifeline of connection and understanding.

One of his letters to her said,

Mendi Mission House

Friday Evening

October 11, 1844

My Dear Sister Harnden,

I said I had thought of you today. Me thought I saw you this morning in Portland making all possible haste to be at the depot in season with your breast heaving with emotion which none but a mother can know.

You are then borne as it were upon the wings of the wind to the embrace of your beloved daughter about to depart on the morrow.

That I will venture to say was the shortest day in your life how every moment was improved! There were great searching of heart that day! A daughter giving up a most affectionate and tender mother and a mother giving up a most beloved daughter for Christ.

What complete prostration and consecration of will to God. Angels with admiration beheld the scene. If there is anything lovely this side of glory, it is such a scene as happened a year ago today---

True, there were very strong maternal and filial affections manifested, and well, there might be – that only added interest to the scene. It showed more clearly the complete victory of the Gospel over nature. Yes, nature in its strongest ties!

Your Brother,

Wm Raymond

Through these letters, he had become intimately acquainted with the heartache etched into Ann's mother's life—the loss of a daughter whose spirit, despite earthly departure, continued to dance among the flowers and soar with the birds of Sierra Leone. It was as if Ann herself had planned the beauty of the day with the help of God. The sun was bright in the sky, and there was a gentle breeze that gently ruffled the sails of the boat moored at the river's edge. The whole village had come down to bid the missionaries a fond farewell. Dressed in their Sunday best, white shirts for the men and soft flowing dresses for the women, they stood on shore waiting for the boat to head out to sea. Porters had loaded all they could take back to America with them. It was time to depart this beautiful land, to say goodbye to the mission house and the many memories it held - both triumphant and sorrowful. Before they would board, Mr. and Mrs. Raymond, along with their children, made one more visit to the patch of land behind the mission house where two primitive crosses marked the resting places of their young son, little George Finney, and their "daughter," Ann Louisa Harnden.

After a short prayer and the laying on of a bouquet of flowers, they headed down to the boat. The Mende children, in deep tribute to the young woman who had changed their lives, sang Ann's favorite hymn,

"O God, Our Help"

"O God, our Help in ages past, our Hope for years to come, our Shelter from the stormy blast, and our eternal Home."

"Under the shadow of Thy throne Thy saints have dwelt secure; sufficient is Thine arm alone, and our defense is sure."

"Before the hills in order stood, or earth received its frame, from everlasting Thou art God, to endless years the same."

As the sounds of the children's voices faded, Mr. and Mrs. Raymond faced their next horizon. The long journey home, the meeting with the Evangelical Society, and the cherished moments they would spend with Ann's mother awaited them at the end of the journey back to America. Holding hands, they quietly prayed for safe and speedy travel.

The decision to meet Ann's mother in person bore the weight of significance. Mr. Raymond, though tethered to the mission's soil, felt the call to venture beyond the familiar horizons. He longed to offer a comforting touch beyond the ink on paper, to share a gaze that transcended the limitations of the written word.

As he stood at the cusp of this journey, the vivid imagery of Sierra Leone became the canvas upon which he painted the essence of the land that had been both witness and accomplice to their collective narrative. In his final conversation with Ann's mother, he chose to recount the beauty that had become inseparable from the memory of her daughter.

Once he was back in Massachusetts, he met with Mrs. Harnden. Mr. Raymond rounded the corner off of Main Street and onto the lane on which Ann's house stood. This short walk was no easier than the voyage to Mende. Filled with uncertainty, his steps slowed as he neared the house. It was a beautiful spring day in New England. The flowers were blooming, the trees budding, and the robins had returned. He thought of the beauty of Mende that they had left behind. Stopping briefly, he gave thanks to God for His creation. Ann's house was set back from the street with a walkway up to the large wrap-around porch lined with spring flowers. A white picket fence in need of some repair stretched across the front yard. The gate creaked as he opened it as if to announce his arrival.

Walking up to the front steps, he saw the old rope swing swaying in the light breeze from the majestic oak that stood to the right side of the home. He could see that the house itself was in need of painting and that the stairs were well-worn.

As he placed his foot on the first step, the front door slowly opened. There in the doorway stood Ann's mother. She appeared tired and worn. Her features carried the weight of loss and pain. With but a nod and slight wave of her hand, she beckoned him to come up and sit on the front porch with her.

Since receiving his letter asking to meet with her, she had been preparing for the encounter. A small tray of iced tea and scones had been set out on a small table between two white wicker chairs. She had tried to envision this meeting but could not; the pain was too great. She had met Mr. Raymond previously, but today, she noticed how he, too, had taken on years from his ordeal in Mende. They sat in silence for a few moments as if to ready themselves for the difficult conversation to come. After taking a sip from her glass, she lifted her eyes to look into his. They both welled up with tears as memories and sorrow overcame them. After gaining his composure, Mr. Raymond apologized for Mrs. Raymond's not being with them. One of their children had taken ill, and she had remained home to care for him. Sister Harndon reached into the pocket of her apron and pulled out the letter she had most recently received from him. With her hand shaking, she placed it on the table next to the scones. The gap between them disappeared. The ocean had once spanned the distance between them, but now that distance was as thin as the paper on which he had penned the words, "Ann has died." She could not help herself and asked him how and why. She had read it in the letter but now needed to hear it from Mr. Raymond's lips. For the next two hours, Mr. Raymond shared the story of Mende Mission and Ann's spirit of love and grace that had inspired so many.

"I have walked amidst the lush landscape of Mende," Mr. Raymond began, his words filled with awe at the land's magnificence and God's artistic hand. "The flowers here unfold their petals in a kaleidoscope of colors. Each bloom, like a brushstroke of divinity, whispers tales of resilience and renewal." In the rhythm of his narration, he conjured the vibrant hues of bougainvillea, hibiscus, and frangipani, each blossom a testament to the intricate craftsmanship of the Creator.

"And the birds," he continued, "oh, how they serenade the dawn and bid farewell to the dusk. Their wings, painted with the hues of the African sky, carry the echoes of a thousand stories. Ann found solace in their songs as if they were choruses of hope echoing across the valleys."

As he spoke, the images of tropical birds, their plumage ablaze with the colors of an artist's palette, fluttered through the conversation. In the intricate dance of nature, he sought to convey the harmonious ebb and flow of life, a dance in which Ann's spirit, though physically absent, remained an integral part.

In recounting the flora and fauna of Sierra Leone, Mr. Raymond wasn't merely describing the external landscape; he was crafting a metaphor for the soul's journey—emerging from the fertile soil of earthly existence, adorned with the vibrant hues of love and faith, and soaring into the boundless skies of eternity.

He recalled special moments he had witnessed between the children of Mende and her daughter. He spoke of her willingness to learn their language and customs and how they laughed when Ann mistakenly called Mr. Raymond a "man of cow" instead of a "man of God." She learned the games they played and excelled at some of them. She often returned to the Mende House in the evening, dusty and dirty from sitting on the ground with the children. The bond she had formed with them was unbreakable. She used this bond to bring them the Gospel message and to tell them about Jesus and His love for them. He was so proud that nearly all the children had surrendered their hearts to God.

He spoke of Ann's care for his wife when she was so ill. He said she was so attentive to his wife's needs that she often paid little attention to her own, skipping meals and staying up through the night.

When little George Finney passed, even when Ann was not feeling well, she gave her all in caring for Mrs. Raymond in the throes of grief. He told Ann's mother he did not believe they could have made it through such a difficult time if it had not been for Ann. When the time came for Mr. Raymand to leave, he took Ann's mother by the hand, and they prayed.

They gave thanks to God for Ann and her life and all the many ways she had blessed both of their lives. Mrs. Harndon called out the two siblings, Mary and her brother George, who were still living at home, to say goodbye to Mr. Raymond. They said their goodbyes and noticed the scones had gone untouched. They asked their mother if they could have them. She said that they certainly could, and they each grabbed one and ducked back into the house to enjoy their special treat.

The final conversation with Ann's mother became a moment of shared memories, of grief and gratitude, of a daughter's lasting impact on a distant land.

Chapter 11: Don't Plan for God

In the dimly lit chambers of the Evangelical Missionary Society headquarters in Massachusetts, Mr. William Raymond, a man weathered by the tropical trials of Sierra Leone, stood before a gathering of his peers. Across the room, Mr. Tappan, the leader of the society, fixed his gaze on Mr. Raymond, anticipation etched on his face.

"Dear brethren," began Mr. Raymond, his voice resonating with a blend of weariness and unwavering resolve, "Our journey to Mende has been a testament to the transformative power of faith and dedication. Allow me to recount the tale of our mission."

As Mr. Raymond unfolded the narrative, the room became a theater of words, transporting the audience to the vibrant landscapes of Sierra Leone. He spoke of families once torn asunder, now reunited in the embrace of their homeland. The chains of ignorance shattered, replaced by the tools of knowledge that laid the foundation for a flourishing community.

"Our endeavor began with the construction of a house, a humble abode that would serve as the beating heart of our mission," Mr. Raymond continued, gesturing animatedly as he described the architectural vision that took form in Sierra Leone. "The walls, though built of earthly materials, echoed with the spirit of a divine purpose."

A murmur of approval and curiosity rippled through the room as Mr. Raymond delved into the construction of the school and church. He spoke of sturdy structures rising against the backdrop of a foreign land, symbols of resilience in the face of challenges.

The school, a sanctuary of learning, echoed with the laughter of children eager to grasp the gifts of education. The church, a sacred space, bore witness to the melodies of hymns that intertwined with the tropical breeze. "In our pursuit, we engaged in delicate negotiations with the king," Mr. Raymond explained, recounting the encounters with the ruler of the Mende tribes. "His majesty recognized the value of our mission, yet harbored concerns about the shifting dynamics within his kingdom." As Mr. Raymond shared snippets of dialogue exchanged with the king, the room hung in suspense, caught between the clash of cultures and the shared aspirations for a harmonious coexistence.

"Our meetings with the king were a delicate dance of diplomacy," Mr. Raymond remarked, his eyes reflecting the complexity of the negotiations. "He struggled with my popularity among his people, a popularity that threatened to overshadow his own influence. Nevertheless, we found common ground in our shared devotion to Christ." The room, now a symphony of hushed whispers, absorbed Mr. Raymond's accounts of cultural nuances and the intricate tapestry of relationships woven in the foreign soil. Dialogue snippets painted a vivid picture of the challenges faced and the compromises forged in the pursuit of a common purpose.

"And so, brethren," Mr. Raymond concluded, his gaze meeting that of Mr. Tappan, "we were granted a year—a year marked by tribulations and triumphs, prayers and hymns. The king, having witnessed the enduring commitment to our mission, has asked us to leave. Change, like the wind, whispers through the very air we breathed in Sierra Leone."

Silence settled in the room as Mr. Raymond's words hung in the air. The essence of their journey, the trials and triumphs, the negotiations and constructions, lingered like a palpable presence in the room. The Evangelical Missionary Society, through Mr. Raymond's narrative, glimpsed the echoes of a mission that transcended borders and left an indelible mark on the fabric of faith and community.

As he continued the narrative of their mission in Mende, his words carried the weight of profound experiences and divine guidance. "Our mission was not solely in the construction of buildings or the establishment of institutions. It was a mission of hearts, a journey where the Christian message flowed like a river, carving its course through the very fabric of Mende." He spoke of the moments when the Gospel resonated through the air, carried by the winds of change that swept through the Mende tribes. "In the midst of unfamiliar tongues and cultural intricacies, the message of

Christ found a home," Mr. Raymond continued, his eyes alight with the fervor of spiritual triumph. "Families gathered under the embrace of newfound faith, and the shackles of spiritual destitution crumbled."

As he recounted the stories of conversions and baptisms, the room became a sanctuary of awe and gratitude. The missionaries, once mere vessels of the divine message, had become witnesses to the transformative power of God's love. "We were but instruments in His hands," Mr. Raymond humbly acknowledged, "and it was His grace that guided us through every step of this extraordinary journey."

In the flickering candlelight, he spoke of nights filled with prayers and hymns that echoed through the Sierra Leonean air. "In the stillness of those moments, we felt the presence of God—His reassuring hand guiding our endeavors, His love enfolding the mission like a protective mantle," Mr. Raymond proclaimed.

The missionaries, their faces reflecting a collective sense of awe, listened as Mr. Raymond painted a tapestry of divine intervention and providence. "In the face of challenges, we found strength in our unwavering reliance on God. His promises became our anchor, and His word our guiding light," he declared, his words weaving a narrative of spiritual resilience.

"As we faced the complexities of cultural nuances and the delicate dance of diplomacy with the king, God was with us," Mr. Raymond testified, his gaze lifted as if seeking affirmation from the heavens. "His wisdom spoke through our words, and His grace softened hearts that were once resistant to the Christian message."

The room, now suffused with a sense of reverence, echoed with whispered praises for the Almighty. "Praise be to God for the success of our mission," Mr. Raymond exclaimed, a deep gratitude infusing his words. "In the midst of earthly farewells, let us not forget the heavenly victories we've witnessed together." His words, a symphony of gratitude and devotion, filled the room. "We stand on the precipice of change, leaving a land enriched by the seeds of Christian love. As we embark on the next chapter, let our hearts resound with praises for the Lord who has been our steadfast companion." The missionaries united in their shared experiences of trials and triumphs, bowed their heads in a collective prayer of thanksgiving. In that sacred moment, surrounded by the flickering candles and the echoes of Sierra Leone, they found solace in the divine assurance that their mission had been blessed by the hand of God.

Mr. Tappan, breaking the silence, spoke with a measured tone, "Brother Raymond, your account of the mission is a testament to the spirit of our society. We may leave one foreign land, but the seeds we've planted there will continue to bear fruit. Let this be a prelude to new territories awaiting the seeds of Christian love."

The room, now stirred with a renewed sense of purpose, began to buzz with discussions of the future. The tale of the Mende mission, a tapestry woven with threads of faith, love, and cultural understanding, had left an indelible mark on the hearts of those gathered in the hallowed halls of the Evangelical Missionary Society.

After the meeting and the feast that was held for the mission's return, Mr. Raymond went to meet Mr. Tappan for a private meeting in a room off the large hall. When he arrived, he was pleased to see former president John Quincy Addams had joined Mr. Tappan. They were having merry conversations, obviously celebrating, as their faces were animated and joyful. John Quincy Adams, a luminary figure in Braintree, Massachusetts, had emerged as the ideal candidate to champion the cause of the Mende Africans before the esteemed chambers of the Supreme Court. His storied past, rich with governmental experience, legal acumen, and an unyielding stance against slavery, had positioned him as the beacon of hope for the captives whose destiny hung in the balance. He would be greatly interested in the mission and its success.

Adams, a Harvard graduate of the class of 1787, entered the legal arena in 1790 after gaining acceptance into the Bar Association in Boston. His early diplomatic forays saw him appointed as the U.S. Minister to Holland by George Washington and later as U.S. Minister to Prussia during his father's presidency. The political trajectory of John Quincy

Adams continued to ascend; after his father's electoral defeat in 1800, he entered the Massachusetts Senate in 1802 and secured a seat in the U.S. Senate in 1803.

The War of 1812 marked a pivotal moment in Adams' career when he skillfully negotiated the Treaty of Ghent in 1814, bringing an end to the conflict. His diplomatic prowess was further showcased during his tenure as Secretary of State under President James Monroe from 1817 to 1825. Adams spearheaded discussions to mend relations with Great Britain, facilitated the acquisition of Florida from Spain, and played a key role in the Transcontinental Treaty, demarcating borders between the U.S. and Spanish territories.

In 1825, Adams ascended to the presidency, advocating for national educational institutions, infrastructure improvements, and comprehensive surveys of the nation's lands.

In February 1841, he passionately argued before the Supreme Court that the Mende were free individuals unlawfully enslaved, advocating for their return to Africa.

The Supreme Court's ruling in favor of the captives marked a triumph for Adams and justice. His immediate communication with co-counsel Roger Sherman Baldwin reflected the gravity of the moment, exclaiming, "The captives are free...Yours in great haste and great joy."

In gratitude, the Mende Africans presented Adams with a Bible in November 1841, expressing their deep appreciation. The accompanying letter, signed by Cinque, Kinna, and Kale, bore witness to their enduring gratitude and prayers for Adams. The symbolic gift served as a poignant reminder of their shared journey and the liberation found through the pages of the holy book.

He had followed the mission closely and was now here to celebrate its first phase. Mr. William Raymond, wearied yet resolute, approached the esteemed figures of Mr. Tappan and John Quincy Adams. Their faces bore a mixture of anticipation and concern, eager to hear the tale of the Mende mission from the man who had led it. "Brother Raymond," Mr. Tappan inquired, his eyes reflecting both curiosity and compassion, "tell us, how fared the mission in Mende? How have the seeds of Christian love taken root in that distant land?"

With a humble nod, Mr. Raymond began his recounting, a narrative that wove together the strands of hardship and triumph. He spoke of the challenges posed by the unfamiliar terrain, the intricate dance of cultural nuances, and the delicate negotiations with the Mende king.

Yet, amidst the trials, the mission stood as a testament to the unwavering resilience of Christian devotion.

"We faced tribulations, brethren, but through God's grace, we persevered," Mr. Raymond declared, his words carrying the weight of divine providence. "The shackles of ignorance were shattered, and souls once adrift found solace in the embrace of divine love. The mission, like a beacon, illuminated the path to salvation for many."

As he spoke of the success of the mission, his gaze lingered on the faces of Mr. Tappan and John Quincy Adams, both pillars of the Christian faith. "The Gospel took root, and many souls were saved," he continued. "The children, once lost in the shadows, found a guiding light in the teachings of Christ. The impact on their lives was profound, a transformation that echoed the triumph of the mission." Mr. Tappan, a man of deep conviction, listened intently. "Praise be to God for the success of the mission," he exclaimed, his voice resonating with gratitude. "His hand has guided us through the trials, and His love has manifested in the lives touched by our endeavors."

The three men returned to the large hall and took in the atmosphere of a deep joy and peace that filled the room. Mrs. Raymond approached her husband, her eyes reflecting a blend of pride and concern. "William," she spoke softly, "tell them of the personal moments. Tell them how this mission was as much for us as it was for the people of Mende. Tell them how God moved in us as well as around us and how He deepened our faith and strengthened our resolve."

With a gentle smile, Mr. Raymond intertwined the broader narrative with glimpses of personal experiences. He spoke of prayers shared under the canopy of starlit African skies, of hymns echoing through the mission house, and the laughter of children filling the air. "In the midst of our service, God graced us with moments of profound connection," he shared, his voice carrying the warmth of cherished memories. Mrs. Raymond, her presence embodying strength and grace, joined the conversation. "The women of Mende welcomed me into their hearts," she expressed, her eyes reflecting the bonds forged in the crucible of shared faith. "Together, we found strength in the Lord, supporting each other through the trials and triumphs of our mission."

The anecdotes painted a vivid picture of a mission not just undertaken in service but lived with a profound sense of purpose and community.

The conversation turned, inevitably, to Ann—their beloved companion on this spiritual journey. "Ann's influence was a gift from God," Mr. Raymond reflected, his voice tinged with both sorrow and gratitude. "Especially on the children, her impact was immeasurable. She nurtured their spirits, and her legacy lives on in the melodies of hymns she taught them."

John Quincy Adams, a man of wisdom and faith, nodded in understanding. "Ann's devotion was a beacon that illuminated the path for us all," he remarked, his words resonating with a shared sense of loss. "Her influence will endure in the hearts of those she touched, and her memory will be a source of inspiration for generations to come. We must all pray for her." Addams addressed the room and told them to gather in prayer for Ann. The flickering candlelight cast a soft glow upon faces marked by both sorrow and reverence. Mr. Raymond, his countenance etched with a mix of gratitude and grief, stood at the forefront, a figure leading this congregation bound by a shared spiritual journey.

As the community came together to lift their voices in prayer, the air resonated with hymns that had once echoed through the very corridors where Ann's laughter lingered. The melodies, a harmonious blend of sorrow and solace, intertwined with the collective breath of those who had witnessed Ann's devotion and felt the impact of her love. Mrs. Raymond, a pillar of strength, stood beside her husband, her eyes reflecting the unwavering faith that sustained them through earthly farewells. The community, both missionaries and Mende believers alike, knelt in unity, forming a circle of hands joined in supplication.

Their prayers, like fragrant incense, ascended to the heavens, carrying with them the collective gratitude for Ann's indelible influence. Each word spoken, each hymn sung, became a testament to the enduring legacy of a woman who had sowed seeds of faith in the fertile soil of Sierra Leone.

Amidst the prayers, testimonies of Ann's kindness and selflessness echoed through the hallowed space. Stories unfolded like petals unfurling in a garden of remembrance—of children nurtured, families united, and souls finding solace in the embrace of divine love. In this sacred gathering, earthly boundaries dissolved, and the community became a tapestry woven with threads of grief and hope. The prayers for Ann's soul became a symphony of voices, an offering of gratitude for a life well-lived in service to God and humanity.

As the echoes of their petitions faded into the stillness, the community left the prayer circle with hearts uplifted, finding comfort in the shared belief that Ann's soul now rested in the eternal embrace of divine love.

A few years later, Mr. and Mrs. Raymond had settled into their new home in Haverhill. His work at the Evangelical Church and their connections with the area had drawn them back to this small New England town. Their new home was sparsely furnished yet quite cozy and welcoming. Mr. Raymond's office was to the right as you entered the front door.

Papers lay scattered on his desk while maps of Africa adorned the wall nearest his chair. He would spend hours in that chair contemplating his travels and praying that God would reveal their next venture. Mrs. Raymond seemed to be past her illness and was doing quite well, although she retained a nagging cough that would come upon her with no notice. The children had grown so much. They loved to play games they learned from the Mende children. One of their favorite games they taught Ann was rolling a wheel with a stick up and down the road, keeping it as straight as they could. One early afternoon, shortly after the children had been put down for their naps, there was a knock on the front door. Mrs. Raymond answered the door, and upon opening it, he was greeted by a young woman who looked rather familiar.

The young woman asked if she could come in and speak with Mr. and Mrs. Raymond. She was invited into the sitting room, and Mrs. Raymond went to her husband's office to bring him to meet her. She went to make some tea while he went into the front room to greet their guest. She stood and looked at him with tears in her eyes.

He was taken aback by how familiar she appeared but could not determine from where. Mrs. Raymond entered with the tea, and they sat down. "Good afternoon, Mr. and Mrs. Raymond," the young woman began, "although we have never met, I feel like I have known you all my life.

My name is Mary, Mary Freedmont." The Raymonds stared, trying to catch some hint of who this woman was. Mr. Raymond was the first to speak, "Welcome to our home, Miss Freedmont. How can we be of service to you? Are you collecting for the local women's organization or for a church?" Mary smiled shyly and opened the top two buttons on her coat to reveal a brooch she wore on the collar of her blouse. It was a beautiful piece, shaped like a robin. "It's Mrs. Freedmont. My maiden's name is Harndon. I am Ann's sister."

The Raymonds could hardly speak. They put their tea cups down, and with tears welling up in their eyes, they stood and reached out to embrace Mary. Ann had often spoken of her lovely sister, who was home helping her mother care for the other children. She had often prayed that God would draw her to Himself and that her heart would be softened so that she could accept Jesus as her Lord and Savior. It took a few moments for them to regain their composure, and then they spent hours talking about the Mission Trip, their love for Ann, and God. When the children woke, Mr. Raymond introduced Ann's sister, Mary, to them. They ran to her, throwing their arms around her neck and holding on as tightly as they could. Mary went on to tell the Raymonds about life in Haverhill after Ann left. It was a real struggle to make ends meet in the household. She worked at the slipper manufacturer in town only to come home and tend to the needs of the children. Her mother could often be found staring out the window in the sitting room that faced east. It took many months for her to be able to function after hearing of the death of her dear daughter Ann. It was shortly after Mr. Raymond's visit that Mary was able to get engaged to a young man from Boston who had done well for himself. He had started his own carpentry shop making cabinets. His name was becoming well known, and they were well off. She would send money to her mother to help her as best she could.

It was just over a year ago that tragedy struck. Her husband was killed in a freak accident in his carpentry shop. Mary was shaking as she told her story, and Mrs. Raymond moved closer and laid her hands upon hers. She found herself in a downward spiral, wishing that life would end for her.

One night, she decided it was time to sell some of her jewelry so that she could get by until it was time to sell the house. In the midst of her jewelry, she found a beautiful little robin-shaped brooch that she had not seen in years.

It was Ann's, returned to her mother in a trunk sent back by Mr. Raymond. Her mother must have snuck it into her things when she moved out.

It all came flooding back. The prayers her mother had prayed over her, the letter she received from Ann pleading with her to give her heart to God. It was there in her room, alone and broken, that she fell to her knees and gave her life to God. Since that time, she joined the local church and was serving wherever she was needed. Like Ann, she loved children and could often be found reading Bible stories to them. Her favorite was the story of Joshua. The scripture, Joshua 1:9, had become her favorite, "Have I not commanded you? Be strong and courageous. Do not be afraid; do not be discouraged, for the LORD your God will be with you wherever you go." Mary was now ready to join the Raymonds in serving the Lord. She had long wanted to come and meet them but had not felt the calling to do so until now. They were not sure what God had in store for them. It had been a few years since their return, and they loved being at home with the children.

Then, in the midst of their conversation, Mr. Raymond stood up and looked into his office at the stack of papers.

He took three long strides to his desk and began to search through the papers he had abandoned to greet his guest earlier.

A letter had arrived yesterday from the Mission Society. He had not yet opened it. He returned to the sitting room and sat on the sofa across from Mary and Mrs. Raymond. He slowly removed the wax seal and unfolded the letter.

Dear Mr. Raymond,

We at the Mission Society have been keeping you and your family in our prayers. We often speak of the night you returned and shared the success of the Mende Mission. We have been in conversation with a few missionaries who have come to New England from out in Pennsylvania. They are putting together a mission trip to Africa. We told them of your mission to Mende, and they are very interested in meeting with you. Would you be available to meet with them next month? May God guide your steps.

Sincerely,

Bertha Reynolds, Secretary

Mr. Raymond let the letter drop into his lap. He slowly raised his eyes to look at the two women across from him. Indeed, God was not finished with the Raymonds and was putting his plan together. The three of them bowed their heads, held hands, and prayed.

© 2024Year Steven M. Darr

All rights reserved. No part of this appendix may be reproduced, distributed, or transmitted in any form or by any means, including photocopying, recording, or other electronic or mechanical methods, without the prior written permission of the author, except in the case of brief quotations embodied in critical reviews and certain other noncommercial uses permitted by copyright law.

For permissions requests or any inquiries, please contact info@stevenm.darr.

This appendix is a collection of personal letters that were transposed by Steven M. Darr and is protected under copyright law. The characters, events, and dialogues in these letters are real.

Thank you for respecting the author's work and intellectual property.

Introduction to Appendix

The following letters have never before been published and available to the general public They were transposed from handwritten letters dating from the 1840's. Many of them survived the journey from Mende, Africa to the United States. Each letter was reviewed a number of times, and where words were ineligible, either the word was omitted or one was inserted with what seemed appropriate in the context.

Letter#1:

Sent from: Ashburnham, Massachusetts

Dated: September 27th, 1843

Miss Ann L. Harnden
Care of Dr. T.M. Martyn
Haverhill, Mass.

Dear Sister Ann,

I received a letter last night from Mr. Tappan. He says there is a vessel leaving from New York around the middle of October. He gives me encouragement to think I shall go in that. I think I shall. He has received a letter from Pres. Mahan written by the direction of the Executive committee of the Evangelical Missionary Society at Oberlin telling him to send me out as soon as they could get enough money to send me and as to my wants after I get there if they are not otherwise supplied, they will supply them. You see the Lord's hand in that.

I received also a letter from my brother in Canada and he cannot go. I have just written to Mr. Tappan telling him that

I think we, by all means, must go - that vessel. I told him we had better take you and go. I expect it will be so. I expect you, Eliza, and I will go together unless the Lord raises up someone we know nothing about. We shall probably go in about three weeks. I told you would have to be ready at a moment's warning. I write you this that you may prepare yourself and be ready. As soon as I get an answer from Mr. Tappan, I will write you and let you know. I cannot tell for certain, but I think you will go. You need not buy any clothes; Mrs. will see to that. Our love to Mr. and Mrs. Martyn and the girls.

Your brother in Christ,

Wm Raymond

    Write me immediately.

Show this to Br. Finney

If you go, I think I shall come to Haverhill after you. Eliz

Letter #2:

Sent from Ashburnham, Massachusetts
Dated: October 5, 1843

Miss Ann L. Harnden
Care of Dr. T. M. Martyn
Haverhill, Massachusetts

Dear Sis Ann,

Yours of the 29th that I received last night. I also received a letter from Mr. Tappan in which he says, "Last evening, the committee met and had a long session. Your letter was read. Also, Miss Harnden's. The committee decided it is best for you, Mrs. Raymond, and Miss H. to leave for Africa this fall." Thus, you see it is decided by the com that you are to go. He says I will inform you as soon as I can when the vessel will sail for Sierra Leone.

You see, the Lord has opened the way for you to go – He has given you favor in the eyes of the community. Isn't this wonderful?

But my dear sister, have you fully counted the cost? It is no small thing to be a missionary. The responsibility…Oh, how awful! Then you have got to leave that dear mother of yours behind – never to hear her kind voice again till it is turned to an angel. Those brothers and sisters, can you say goodbye? Then there are all your Christian friends. There are all the comforts- not to say luxuries- of civilization. There is a prospect of living while you do, live a single life, have you thought of that? There is a prospect of sickness, amongst strangers, amongst heathen – perhaps death. Have you counted the cost?

You will have trials that you now cannot conceive of? You must find the witness that God has called you continually. I don't know when the vessel will sail. I will let you know as soon as I find out. I think likely it will start in two or three weeks. You had better send for your mother immediately. You will not have too much time to see her. Go to work and make all the preparations necessary immediately. I think I shall go to Boston next week, and perhaps I may go to Haverhill and see how you get along.

Your brother in great haste,

Wm Raymond

Letter #3:

Sent from New York, New York

Dated: October 5, 1843

Miss Ann L. Harnden

Haverhill, Massachusetts

Dear Friend,

Mr. and Mrs. Raymond are very desirous that you should accompany them to Africa to assist in their labors on behalf of the Mendi Mission, and it appears by your letter to Mr. Raymond, dated August 6th, which he put into my hands, that you are very desirous of going.

The executive committee of the Union Missionary Society has decided to accept your proposition and to aid you in your benevolent enterprise.

They wish you health, the opportunity of doing good in the vineyard of the Lord and the (unable to read), and blessing of the Lord of the vineyard.

Very truly and (unable to read) yours,

Lewis Tappan

(Corresponding Secretary)

Letter #4:

Sent from New York, New York

Dated: October 23, 1843

Mrs. Hannah Harnden

Dear Madam,

As you will be pleased to hear of your daughter Ann Louisa's safe and pleasant departure for Africa, I take an early opportunity to write to you.

Mr. and Mrs. Raymond and your daughter passed a few days here quite pleasantly. We had the pleasure of seeing them at my home, and a public meeting was held in one of the churches. They made many friends here. At the conclusion of the public meeting, they stood under the pulpit while a large number of the congregation came and took them by the hand. Many of the sisters in Christ who were present gave Mrs. Raymond and your daughter also a parting kiss.

Saturday at 2 o'clock was the time finally set by the owners of the Brig Frances Lord for the departure. The vessel was at anchor half a mile from the city in the North River. Mr. and Mrs. Raymond and your daughter went off in a boat a little after one. When it was nearly two o'clock, I went on board. The wind blew fresh, and it was ahead. I found our friends snugly situated. The Brig is a neat vessel – the cabin is convenient, and your daughter has a stateroom wholly to herself opposite Mr. and Mrs. Raymond. Everything on board looked comfortable. Captain Brown is considered a good seaman. I expressed a hope that he would be very kind to Mr. and Mrs. Raymond and your Ann Louisa, and I have much to believe he will.

We have supplied our friends with every necessary thing for the passage to Africa, and for their maintenance and comfort after their arrival.

The steamboat took the Brig down the Harbor soon after I left. Yesterday the wind changed and blew fresh. This morning a young man who lives with McCracken and Livingston, merchants here who have sent the Brig out, called to tell me that he left the Brig at the narrows, that she went to sea immediately – the wind having changed a little. I suppose by this time – one o'clock Monday they are 300 miles from land. The wind is fair and the weather pleasant.

Mr. Raymond sent up a farewell letter by the young man, and I will make an extract for you.

On - *"Brig Frances Lord"* near Sandy Hook

Dear Brother Tappan,

"We are all in good spirits. Everything thus far is very pleasant and there is a suspect of a very pleasant voyage. Our accommodations are very good.... Sister Harnden is in excellent spirits and rejoices in the privilege of leaving her native country for the sake of the Gospel."

They will probably have about 58 days to Sierra Leone, and one may expect to hear from them in about four months. The Brig will stay on the coast sometime trading and getting a return cargo. Perhaps we shall not hear from our friends until the return of this Brig.

I rejoice that you have a daughter who is disposed to undertake such a voyage for the Savior's sake. It is true you had but a little time to be with her after she had made up her mind to go, but I trust you are one of those who consider your children, and all you have, as belonging to the Lord and are willing to surrender them at His call, however sudden. Abraham, you know, did not have so long notice as you did. If your daughter's life is spared, I trust she will do much good to the benighted heathen. If she shall early be called away it will be because our blessed Savior wills it. Let us commit ourselves and our children into His hands unreservedly. May He comfort and bless you abundantly.

Should I receive intelligence, I shall hasten to communicate it to you, and it will give me pleasure to hear from you at all times. If you move to your place of residence, please let me know, as in case of a good opportunity to send to Africa, I shall wish to send you letters. Owing to the liberality of many friends of this mission, the committee have been able to provide liberally for the wants of our friends. I trust that while the committee prays for your daughter and yourself, you will remember them when you go to the throne of grace.

With much regard, your brother in the Lord,

Lewis Tappan

Letter #5:

Extract from a letter from Gambia,

Dated: November 22, 1843

To Mrs. Hannah Harnden

Georgetown, Mass

Arrived here last night. We have had a remarkable passage; we were only 30 days from New York. We have had not only a short but a remarkably pleasant passage. The time has passed very rapidly away. We have had no gale and no bad storm the whole passage.

The vessel has been very comfortable and pleasant our fare has been good. The captain is a pleasant and gentlemanly man.

We all acknowledge his kind treatment. We had a very agreeable company. We had prayers every morning in the cabin (by ourselves) except one, and services every Sunday after the first.

There has been but one unpleasant circumstance since we left New York. (With the exception of a man falling overboard but who was saved.) and that was this. A few days ago, the second mate put a very improper note into sister

Harden's stateroom window. She showed it to the captain, who immediately called the mate and told him not to show himself in the cabin again. In this the captain showed himself a gentleman.

We are all well and in excellent spirits. We are more and more satisfied that Sister Harnden is called of God to the work. She is more and more endeared to us we are indeed a happy few.

I cannot fail to mention the great kindness of the Wesleyan Missionaries here. I saw a man from Freetown. He was at York a short time since.

He says, "The people of York cry to see you." I will write more fully from Sierre Leone. My confidence in the success of the mission grows stronger and stronger. I have enjoyed the most blessed communion with my heavenly father.

I have learned much about this blessed Gospel. My little soul seems to expand more and more every day.

There is a meaning in the word communion that I never realized so fully as now. I feel I need not ask you to pray for us. I need wisdom – much wisdom.

My wife never enjoyed such communion with God in her life as since we left New York. We find Sister Harnden indeed a most blessed sister.

She is one of the chosen of the Lord. She is very happy and has enjoyed much of the presence of her God on the passage.

In haste your brother,

Wm Raymond

Letter #6:

**Written at sea by Ann Harnden aboard the Frances Lord
Dated: November 1843**

My very dear Mother,

I have just sat down with the intention of writing to you, thinking perhaps I should have an opportunity to send it before I get to Sierra Leone. As we are going to stop in the Gambia, oft, dear mother, have I looked back upon the American shores, oft have I fancied myself there holding sweet communion with you and with our god. How sweet would be the reality! But our Father has otherwise ordered and I did not wish to complain. Complain! Did I say? This, to one, is an almost unmeaning word. So, far from feeling anything of a complaining spirit, I feel to thank God that things are just as they are. I would not have a thing altered for the world. Not that I should not like to see you if I could, for it would rejoice my heart to see you. But because my father has called and I do not feel (like Lots' wife) to look back with a longing wish to return. I feel the "witness" that God has called me brighter than ever. I cannot doubt it.

I believe I shall have cause to bless God throughout eternity, that He had called me to the great work of laboring in His vineyard in Africa, unfit as I am to perform all that He requires me to do. It appears to me I never saw myself so infinitely unworthy and incapable of doing anything from the cause. I have given myself to work. I have often thought if God has chosen some other one more capable than myself, it seems as though they might do something – in the sphere to which I have been called. It seems to me I can do nothing at all, and I cannot of myself, but this had been a most blessed passage to me, "through Christ strengthening me, I can do all things." I can go forward in the strength of this promise feeling I can daily ask for that wisdom which comes from God who giveth all men liberally. Knowing that whatsoever I ask in faith, I shall receive.

And now, my dear mother, how do you feel in your soul? Do you feel to thank God that you have been instrumental in raising up a child of yours to carry the Gospel to the heathens? Do you feel to praise Him that he has called your child ____ that he has called her to go far from you and that he has sundered those endearing ties that bind our hearts together? Or do you feel that all of these things are against you and that you cannot have it so? And that your burden is greater than you can bear? Or, as you said before, I came away to me that you had rather bury me? It seems to me, dear mother, you do not realize what you were, or if you did, that you were not in the right state of mind. You said if I were dead, you should know that I was not suffering. Was that the right spirit? Ought you not be willing to rejoice that God has counted me worthy to suffer for the sake of Christ? I have often thought how I should like to have you look in upon us and see how comfortable we are. We have a pleasant vessel – a pleasant captain and pleasant weather. Mr. and Mrs. Raymond are very kind to me – they could not be kinder if I were their own child. But what is better than all the rest, our heavenly Father is with us bearing us onward to the port of our destination. When I realize that it is my own dear mother that I am addressing, I is a wonder to myself that I can write to you not knowing as I ever shall see you again on earth and not be almost overwhelmed in tears. I know I could not without the help of God. Oh! What a blessing we have got. How true it is that He will enable us to perform all that He requires of us to do.

Christ says, "He that loveth father or mother more than me is not worthy of me and he that loveth son or <u>daughter</u> more than me is not worthy of me."

Now my dear mother, if you love me more than Christ and His cause, He says you are not worthy of Him. If you love Him, I think you will rejoice because I leave you for Christ. He has promised to be with you and sustain me and not only to provide for the body but to provide for the soul. He says that "Every one that hath forsaken houses or brethren or sisters or father or mother or wife or children of lands for my name's sake shall receive a hundred-fold and shall inherit everlasting life." Matt 19:29.

Now dear mother, are you not willing that I should leave you to carry the Gospel to those who are setting in the region shadow of death if by so doing I can be used as an instrument in the hands of God in turning one sinner from the error of his ways to serve the living and true God? God has promised to be for me and if God be for me, who can be against me? But if I had none of these promises, could you bear the thought of my staying with you when I have the <u>witness</u> that God has called me to go to Africa?

And should I refuse to go just because it was so hard? For me to part with my dear mother and my much beloved brothers and sisters and my dear friends? Would this, think you, be an excuse that would stand me in a dying hour that because I loved my friend so much better than Christ and His cause? I could not bear than to be separated a little while (for this life is but short at its longest) in laboring in His vineyard.

Me thinks I hear you answer not. No, my dear mother God forbid that you should be guilty of such thoughts and that I should be guilty of such conduct. It seems to me I can read your thoughts at this moment. You used to say the Lord's will be done. But is the Lord's will your will? Do you feel that you are entirely consecrated to God? Do you feel that if He should call another of your dear children to labor in a distant part of His vineyard that you could part with that one also and not only feel to say the will of the Lord be done but to rejoice in that will. If these are not your feelings, I fear you are not in the state of mind God wants you to be in.

Christ knew the feeling of a mother. He knew the feelings of a daughter. In fact, there are no friends so near but he knows how dear they are to our hearts.

When He said, "Go unto all the world and preach the Gospel to every creature." What a blessed thought it is that there is no place in which we can be placed so trying that Christ can't sympathize with us. He has been tempted in all points _____ _____ are and He knows how to succor those that are tempted. You may ask what temptations has to do with my going to Africa. To answer you, I want to say they have now much to do with me and I should think you strong if the devil has not been harassing you about it. He has brought up everything before my mind that he could to try to make me to believe that God had not called me. But I have looked to God and

He has delivered me out of all his temptations. It seems to me that if I had stayed with you or anywhere in the United States and had not gone to Africa, I would have been one of the most unhappy of creatures on the earth. I would have been a source of trial to you, to myself, and to all around me.

But now I am as happy as I can be. I sometimes think that perhaps you will think I have lost all love for you, but it is not so. The more I think of you, the more I love you, and the more I love my heavenly Father for having given me a Christian mother to train me for the service. For had you, dear mother, been an opposer to religion, I should not have been where I am now unless God had as, by miracle, snatched me as a brand from the burning. It was the impressions I received from you in my childhood that first led me to look at myself as a lost sinner and to pray to God for forgiveness. How often, dear mother, did you tell me to be a good girl and to pray to God to make me good? The words 'good girl' went to my heart. I would often think of the advice of my dear mother, and the commandment "children obey your parents in all things" would come home to me.

I felt I was continually disobeying you, not only you but God for I knew I could not be good so long as I was in rebellion against God, and I could not bear to think of disobeying that mother I loved so well. I knew I loved you and wanted to obey you, so I prayed to God to forgive me and after a long struggle with unbelief, I was led to trust in Christ and found peace in believing. You may think it strong that I should write this now, but I do it to encourage you to continue to be faithful to the cause of Christ and to your remaining children, and because my attention has been called to the importance of persevering in prayer and in our labors to save souls.

When you feel your heart drawn out by the Spirit of God to pray for a soul, I believe you are bound to persevere in prayer and exercise faith that God will save that soul. You may know that you are led by the Spirit if your heart is drawn out in love.

Now, dear mother, when you begin to think you can do nothing think of that one word that God used to put me upon thinking about my soul. I believe I have learnt some new lessons about these things myself and this is the reason why I write them to you. I don't know if you have already learnt them. If you have, you will be glad to know that I have. I wish also that you may be encouraged to pray for Mary. I believe she will yet be a child of God. The other children too. I must say here that I have felt very differently from what I ever did before about Mary. I believe she will yet be a child of God. I believe it will be for the glory of God to save her, but I know He will not save her contrary to her own will. I believe she will yet see the error of her ways and turn to God and live (torn page). I know that Christ's blood is sufficient to cleanse from all sin.

Letter #7:

Sent from New York

Dated: January 29, 1844

Dear Madam,

I have received two letters from Rev. William Raymond, dated in Africa. They had a very pleasant passage. The captain was quite civil and attentive; the accommodations were good; the provisions were ample; and they had religious privileges. But I think you will be pleased to have extracts from the letters. We rejoice to have such good news. The Gambia River is about 300 miles north of Sierra Leone. It would not take them long to run down to that place.

I remain very truly and respectfully your friend,

Lewis Tappan

Letter #8:

Sent from: Kaw Mendi, Sherbro, West Africa

Dated: April 22, 1844

My Dear Sister,

I have often caught my pen and scratched a line to you since I left America but have never written you in full as I have wished. Time has prevented this. I will try to do it now, though my time is now, very precious, having a great deal on my hands. What I have written before I hardly can recollect; therefore, should I repeat some things that I have written, you must not be impatient though it is now six months since I heard you say "goodbye" - yet not a word have I heard from you since. I have been anxious to hear from you for many reasons and if anyone was more prominent than another it was that I might know how your mind was in reference to Ann's leaving you. The day she left you was a trying day for your soul. All the tenderest feelings of a loving mother of a beloved child were brought into action. I was a father once and I imagined your feelings. I thought I saw a struggle, a heavy struggle between nature and grace – the mother and the Christian. Nature said I could not give her up, but Grace said I could. It was a severe struggle, and whether the heart took the attitude of rebellion or not, I could not tell. There was an expression that escaped your lips and complete subjection as they should have been. It struck me with peculiar forthcoming from one in whose piety, I had so great confidence. It was this you "said," you had rather follow Ann to the grave than see her go to Africa. This was an outbreak of a mother's feelings. It was doubtless but the impress of the moment. Time has doubtless led you to look at all things in their right light. That day is a memorable day for you. It is so to me. It is so to me not only because I wept to see you weep but because you then threw upon me all the responsibilities of a father. Often have I seen you stand as you stood that day before me with weeping lips, charging to me to watch over Ann as a father. I have felt like a father to her; I think she has felt like a child.

Ann, as a general thing, has been very happy since she left you, though she has not been without her trials and some of them severe indeed. Our passage out was, on the whole, very pleasant. I think I never enjoyed more of the presence of my Savior than there. I felt the charge you had given me, I felt that Ann possessed the most tender feelings and leaving her mother and all her friends, I felt she needed the kindest treatment from me. I treated her accordingly. I am not aware that my conduct toward her was such that you or any other Christian could disapprove. Nothing of an unpleasant nature happened till two or three days before we arrived in Zambia. The second mate then put into Ann's state room window the following note for reasons too plainly indicated in the note itself.

> *"If you want to hear something that will be greatly to your advantage, come on deck at 1 o'clock tonight. For that will be the time that I shall be on deck. Do not be afraid, I will pledge you, my honor. Don't show this to anyone. If you do it will ruin me. If you will come slip a note into my cabin the first chance you get and you shall hear of something that will be more to your advantage than you are aware of."*

You know enough of Ann to know how she felt upon receiving such a vile note as this. She brought the note to me. I need not say she wept. As soon as the second mate found that I knew it, he called me and begged me to say nothing about it till we got to Sierra Leone and then he would make all things plain to her. We did not think best however to say nothing about it. Ann gave the note to the captain and the 2nd mate was immediately (cannot make out) out of the cabin and never came in there again the rest of the passage when the captain was on board. Being turned out of the cabin, as a matter of course, did not please him. When we arrived in Sierra Leone, he circulated a report like the following. That he had seen me go into Ann's state room in the night, etc., etc., etc., As soon as I heard of it, I went to the captain and asked him if he saw anything improper in my conduct toward Ann. He said no. I asked the mate; he said no. I called Mr. Jones who is at the head of the church Mission and Mr. Dove who is at the head of the Wesleyan mission, and all went on board to look into the matter. The 2nd mate said he was ready to take his oath that he saw me go into Ann's stateroom in the night and stay one and a half by the watch. Notwithstanding that his statements were so disconnected and the reasons he gave for writing this vile note so absurd and ridiculous that both Mr. Jones and Mr. Dove were fully satisfied that the whole was a made-up lie. Mr. Jones advised me to prosecute him for defamation of character. This I did not wish to do. I wish to have nothing to do with law. We finally concluded it was best for Mr. Dove and Mr. Jones to write joint letters stating their views on the matter. They did so.

They said in their letter, "After careful investigation, we come to the deliberate conclusion that there was not the slightest foundation for the abominations imputed to Mr. Raymond which seemed the effects of surmise, and we cannot but think prejudice to the anti-slavery cause."

This letter was directed and sent to Dr. Tappan. I had no doubt that the report would reach home and would be caught hold of by the enemies of the mission. And I felt it was my duty to send him an (unreadable). The probability is both the report and the letter have been published before this. Perhaps you may have seen it and wondered that Ann has never said anything about it in her letters to you. The reason is this. At first, she did not wish to write about it for fear it would worry you, and then it became an old story to her, and for this reason, she did not write about it. I need not say this was a very severe trial for us all, but especially for Ann. But the Lord carried us all through it and sustained us in a wonderful manner. This affair kept us much longer in Freetown than we intended to stay. We moved to York, where we stayed till the 12th of March. Regarding the particulars of our moving, Ann has written to you from time to time. It will take hours for me to take time and paper to repeat them. Ann has had and still has many trials such as are common to the missionary.

It is no small thing to be a missionary. She has been sick and had no physician to administer medicine. No friend, mother, or sister to watch over her to smooth her pillow or to cool her burning brow. My wife was unwell at the time and hardly able to take care of herself. I tried the best I could to act the part of 'father', but I did not mind. I was rather clumsy and awkward about it. I took care of her night and day; I was both a physician and nurse. But very few have the fever so lightly as she had. It was very high, however, for two or three days, and had she been under a regular physician's care, she doubtless would have been stuffed with calomel, and it would have gone much worse with her as it was on the bed for about 10 days.

She, afterward, while I was away from home, had an attack of the ague and fever, which lasted about a week. Since she has been home, she has had another attack which lasted about the same time. Notwithstanding this she is by far more fleshy than when she left home. She is unable to wear the dresses she had when she left home except such as she has altered.

She was weighed the other day and she weighed 120 pounds. Her health, as a general thing, has been very good. With it above expectations. She says she has learned one thing, and that is "A contented mind is a continual feast," and this, she says, is what makes her so fleshy. You may pity us living as we do in a floorless mud house, but I doubt whether you will find another as happy a family all the world over. You must not think that while we are deprived of some of the better comforts which you enjoy, we are suffering or unhappy. No, far from that. We sometimes wish you with us for a short time to share in our enjoyment. Our enjoyments are not of a sensual character. They are the enjoyments of the soul of that nobler part of our being. As a family, we are bound together with love, and as a family, we are bound by the same Lord of love to the very throne of God. We are living day by day with the abiding witness of full consecration God is with us. Our seasons of family prayer are blessed seasons. Day by day, our hearts are melted together into one presented to God as a living sacrifice that we feel is acceptable to Him. In the morning, our practice is to read one or two chapters of the Bible by reading all around, then we sing a hymn, and then my wife and I pray. I wish you could look in upon us at one of these seasons. We have services twice on the Sabbath besides Class Meetings.

Many things which Ann at first thought would be a trial proved to be no trial.

While I am writing this, she is sitting with a naked child, some 9 or 10 months old, in her lap. Scarcely a day passes over, but you will see her folding the little naked creatures in her arms. Every day you see, in our house, little boys – five or six years old and perfectly naked - are running and playing about. Nothing suits Ann better than to get some of these boys around her and learn from them the names of things in the Sherbro language or tell them the names of things in English. After having said what I have I need not say. Ann is happy and contented. She had learned much about the great and glorious scheme of redeeming love since she left you. She had been growing in knowledge and in grace. I do not mean to be understood when I say we are so happy that we have no trials. But they only help us on our way.

Living as we do in the King's public house or palace, as Ann is pleased to call it, we are sometimes very much annoyed with the King's company. For instance, a week or two ago, a neighbor, the King, made the old man a visit. Well, we had to have them all at our house to eat. We had to set our table for 10 or 12. But it is an old saying that it is an ill wind that blows not any good. The old man killed a bullock and gave us nearly a quarter. We have the King to eat with us all of the time. I have been very troubled to get hands to assist in building my house. So, I am not as far advanced as I had wished, but I am in the hope of getting it done before the rains set in hard. I have now about 20 men at work on it.

The prospects of the mission never were so encouraging as at present. You know that I always look on the bright side of the picture, but things are better than ever. I expect I do not think I shall have any trouble in getting plenty of children for our school. I do not think I shall be able to have a school built before the rains come on. I shall hardly be able to have a school before the next dry season, which will commence in November. You are now going to have your summer but we, our winter.

The spot on which our mission house is to be built is indeed beautiful. It is situated some 10-12 rods from the river. The land gently descends all of the way to its bank. The scenery is beautiful. The land about is beautiful- studded with palm trees that lift up their heads far above the surrounding bush. Infront is a beautiful river about half as wide, I should judge, as the Merrimac at Haverhill. The opposite side is lined with a beautiful evergreen whose leaves resemble the palm. Unequaled by anything I ever saw in America. It doubtless looks more beautiful to me than anybody else from the fact I feel it is the very spot to which my God has sent me. To me, it looks almost like a little paradise. And the more I look at it the more I am pleased with it. But stop this. My health is very good. You would think so should you see my day-by-day hold of the ax, the hoe, the shovel, or whatever tool the work may require. My health is better than when in America. Eliza's health is better than it was in America, but now it is not very good. She expects to be confined in July, and I expect that will be a very trying time with her. It will be in the middle of the rainy season at the very time when Europeans are most likely to have a fever. Should fever set in at that time, I should have no hopes of her life. My trust, however, is in the Lord who delivered us this far. Remember us in prayer. We do not forget you. May the same God that is with us be with you. Eliza sends her love.

Your brother in Christ,

Wm. Raymond

Letter #9:

Sent From: Mendi Mission House

Dated: August 9, 1844

A scrap written on the day of Ann's funeral.

And is it so? Must I, can I believe it? Is it true? It must be, though my mind cannot realize it. It is true. I sat upon her bedside and held her hand in mine, and watched her flickering breath to the last. These hands of mine closed her eyes in death. These same hands put upon her the robe of death. They made her a narrow house and helped put her into it. I have knelt by the side of her grave and heard that hollow sound which came from thence. It is true Ann is dead. I look into her room – it is desolate. A death-like silence reigns through the house. There seems to be something wanting. Our family seems like a watch that has lost one of its principal wheels.

Last night I threw my wearied body upon my bed to rest. Sleep, I would not. Hark! I thought I heard that sweet voice softly say, "Maria" as it used to speak it. I started up in my bed. But ah! How mistaken true those lips were there but they were locked in death. *(Maria was particularly her girl. She always stayed in her room when I was not there and slept there when I did not)*

As I now sit to write, I cast my eyes out of the door and behold a newly made heap of earth. It was not there this morning. Beneath that heap of earth… this hat belongs to the one we loved – but stop. Why am I so groveling? Why am I diving down to the bottom of the grave when our sister is not there? Why not rather follow that cloud of angels that brought her ransomed spirit to the mansion prepared for it? Lord, give me faith, and I will try. Let us step back to yester morn. That was a silent, solemn hour. Tears were she then. When shall I forget it? "Let my right hand forget her cunning, and my tongue cleaves to the roof of my mouth; in that day, death was there, but he had no sting. Look! Who are these?

"Bright angels have from glory come

They're round her bed, They're in her room

They wait to waft her spirit home"

With me, they watch the fleeting breath. It is done. The struggling spirit is free. It has escaped from death's embrace, mounts on angel's wings, and is borne upward away. Where I sat watching to see if there was to be still another gasp, she had already reached those pearly gates – already had entered those golden streets. Hark! Do you hear? Heaven's hallelujahs receive a new impulse. They grow higher and higher still, another ransomed soul safe in glory. Bring hither the crown of gold, the white robe, and the golden harp.

Glory, honor, praise, and power be unto the Lamb forever. Hallelujah, Amen.

She is now crowned a king, priest unto her God forever. Me thinks I see her now. She approaches the throne and casts her crown at the feet of Him, who sits upon it. Hark! Do you hear those sweet, those heavenly – those glorious strains which flow from off that harp? Did you think our "Little" sister Ann could ever make such music – How sweet- how ravishing. My own soul begins to catch the flame.

> *"I want, oh I want to be there*
>
> *I want to be one of your choir*
>
> *And turn my own harp to His praise."*

William Raymond

Letter #10:

Sent from: Mendi Mission House

Dated: August 10, 1844

Today, the mission boat is on her way from Sierra Leone and is winding her way up the crooked river to the mission house. They are a mile or two below – they meet a canoe. "What news?" they inquire. One word is spoken, and the boatman's arms are paralyzed.

The oars lie motionless or but faintly perform their duty. What was that word which had such magic power? It was this, "Miss Ann is dead."

I meet them at the wharf. All is still. Scarce a word is spoken. My soul is full. My coxswain, "Daddy George," comes on shore. I take his hand in mine but cannot speak. He was the first one with whom I had met since Ann's death to whom I could open my soul, and now my heart forbade me utterance.

We walked in silence together to the house; I took him to the back door and pointed to the grave and think I said, "Yesterday," and turned away.

When I opened my package of letters there were two for Ann. My feeling can better be imagined than described as I looked upon those letters.

That she had lived to receive these letters. But then I thought, "She now knows a great deal more about her friends than these letters could tell her. Her swift spirit has (torn page) this visited her mother, brothers and sisters and friends and knows all about their state and welfare."

William Raymond

This, although dated August 10th, was written September 1st. This I learned a few days ago by having one of the boatmen tell the girls about it on September 1st.

We called her "Miss" Ann in our family, and she was called so by the boat's men and by all the people. I do not think the people knew that she had any other name but "Miss Ann."

WR

My coxswain George Hayes, or as we always call him, "Daddy George," who is a very devoted Christian, thought a great deal of Ann, and so did she of him and of his wife "Mommy Mary," who is also a devoted Christian.

Daddy George used frequently to go into Ann's room and talk with her about things pertaining to the Gospel. He never prayed in the family without praying for her. He generally prayed something as follows, "Lord, have mercy upon sister Ann.

Built her up in the most holy faith, strength her- thou knowest the afflict of her body. Send a doctor from heaven." On one occasion, he prayed, "Lord, have mercy on our "little" sister Ann." That is the reason why I use the word "little" in the above. Why he used it I don't know. It pleased me at the time, and I think I spoke to Ann about it.

WR

Letter #11:

Sent from: Mendi Mission House, Little Boom River Sherbro, West Africa

Dated: August 25th, 1844

My Dear Sister Harnden,

I have been led to think much of you of late and now sit down to write you. Where to begin, I know not. It is painful to be the bearer of unpleasant news, but especially so when we ourselves are in the affliction. To come to it at once, that beloved daughter of yours whom you so freely devoted to God, He has taken to Himself. It is true though I can hardly make myself believe it. Ann is dead. She died about 9 o'clock on Thursday morning, August 8th. I did not think her immediately dangerous till a few days before she died. You may be ready to say that her death was caused by the unhealthy climate. Maybe it was, but her disease was one I never have known before in this country. Inflammation of the stomach. This, I think, was produced by another, which is peculiar to her sex. It will doubtless be gratifying to you to know all the particulars from the very beginning. I will try to give them to you, though in doing it, you will have to excuse me for speaking of some things that under other circumstances would be a breach of propriety. I write you as her "father" and her physician. While in New York, when it was with her after the "manner of women," she took a very heavy cold. She thought at the time and has always thought that it did not materially impair her. I do not know that it did, but I have been led to think, since her death, that perhaps that was the foundation of her disease. Be this as it may, she was not "unwell" again till January, when she had the seasonal fever.

This fever was caused more by the obstruction of the menses than it was by the climate. As soon as she was relieved of this, this fever left her, and she enjoyed comparatively good health for some time. But as a matter of course, she could not go long without being "regular." Shortly after our removal to Kaw Mendi, which was about the middle of March, she again had a fever under the same circumstances as before.

After she had got about from the fever again about the first of May, as near as I can remember, she was taken with awful distress in her stomach, which lasted about an hour. What to do for her, I knew not. I gave her several things suitable to relieve colic, but they did no good. At her request, I gave her some Cayenne pepper tea. This relieved her immediately.

From that time, she frequently complained of that distress in her stomach. On the 20th of May, she was taken with inflammation of the bowels. I should have said, however, that she was sick most of the time- from the time she had that distress in her stomach till this time- though not always confined to her bed.

For the inflammation in the bowels, I applied a large blister over the stomach and bowels, but the plaster had been so long in the country that its strength was lost, and it did not make a blister much larger than a mini penny. I then put a mustard poultice just as large as the blister plaster. This produced the desired effect. This disease, as a matter of course, reduced her strength.

On Sunday night, May 26th, all of the fore part of the night, she was so weak that I was obliged to lift her up in bed so that she might take a drink of water. About midnight my wife had the symptoms of approaching labor. Ann, though so weak, under the excitement of the moment, got up and dressed herself, and when the child was born, which happened about 4 o'clock in the morning- she washed and dressed it. Before she got it done, she sunk perfectly exhausted on the bed.

On Tuesday night, she was taken with a kind of palsy. She lost all use of her legs, arms, and sometimes of her tongue. It also affected her mind making her stupid. I could not give her a drink of water without holding her by main strength. The next day after Ann was taken with this palsy, my wife was taken with a most violent diarrhea. She lost all power over her discharges and lay like a perfectly helpless infant in bed. Thus, I had at one time two perfectly helpless women and a premature child three days to wash and dress and feed with the spoon all at the same time. This was the steepest place in which my god ever placed me. On one occasion, while I was attending to my wife, I heard a noise in Ann's room.

I went in and found her prostrate on the floor. My wife got better so that the next week, she nursed the child, though she was not able to. She nursed it till it was two weeks old and then sunk down completely exhausted and never has been well or in her right mind since. By this time, Ann had got so much better that she took the child and took care of it for one week. She was again completely prostrated. Again, I had the two sick women and the child on my hands and continued to have till God took the little one to Himself which happened when it was about five weeks old.

Ann suffered so very much from constipation of the bowels. Seldom for two months before she died did she have an evacuation of the bowels without being produced by a physic. As soon as her bowels became constipated, she would be troubled with the palsy as soon as her bowels were moved, she was relieved of that.

She suffered much from vomiting and retching, especially when constipated. I do not think she suffered much pain only from the retching. She used frequently to say to me as she lay in bed that she felt perfectly well. Her appetite, I should have said, became very poor, and what little she did eat, she would frequently vomit up. I looked forward to the time when we should move to our own house as a time when she would begin to mend.

We moved to our house on Tuesday, July 16th, and instead of gaining, she failed from that day till she died. The day we moved was somewhat damp, and she probably took cold. After she came, she was so strong that by my assisting her, she walked about the house to see it and was much pleased with it. The day we moved she was under a great deal of excitement and was more or less delirious ever after. After our removal, her bowels remained constipated as before.

She could not take physic and could not for some time before we moved, for as soon as she took it, she would vomit it up. I tried and tried again, first one thing and then another, till I became discouraged.

I felt there was but one thing which I did not try and that was an injection and that I felt propriety would not allow me to administer. I say her bowels remained constipated and I could not relieve them. Her appetite failed altogether so that it was with difficulty that I could prevail on her to take a little gruel.

The retching increased. Vomit she could not, for she had nothing she could vomit except now and then a little bile. You can easily see under these circumstances that she must quickly fade away. It was painful indeed to me to see her under these circumstances and I could not assist her in any way. I became satisfied her disease was inflammation of the stomach. My medicine book describes the disease and leaves it there by saying that its "management required the highest order of medical skill." I thought I would try a mustard poultice on her stomach.

This seemed but to hurry on the work of destruction. I tried some strengthening bitters which I had for a few days to see if it would not create an appetite, but I thought it hurt her and left it off. I tried Quinine for two days and left it off for the same reason. I had now nothing to do but to keep her comfortable and see her waste away.

For three weeks before she died, I do not think she ate a pint of this gruel. I used to make it generally twice a day and carry it to her and ask her if she wished to eat some then her general answer was "Wait a little I am very tired now." In the course of the day, I could prevail on her to take two or three spoons full.

For four days before she died, she never put anything but water in her mouth. On Wednesday morning the morning before she died, I asked her how she did. She whispered "Better" I asked her if she wanted something to eat. She nodded her head. You can easily imagine the thrill that went to the bottom of my soul at the word "better", and with what speed I made some gruel. When I brought it, she was "tired" and could not eat. For two or three days before she died, she was taken with almost incessant purging and "flooding". It was at this time that my hopes began to give up. I had for a long time consider her case as a dangerous one, but I did not till now consider her in imminent danger.

I know now there must be a change very soon for better or for worse. For some time, previous to her death, I had one girl "Maria" sit in the room all of the time to give her water and hold her head when she retched.

I used to go in every little while myself to see if she wanted anything. I slept by the side of her bed at night. On the morning she died, I perceived she was insensible and did not breath so freely. I did not think she was so near her end. I sat upon the side of bed and looked at her and thought to myself, "Well it is not impossible, but God may even now raise you.

My dear wife has been to all appearances lower than you and God raised her up." I left her bedside and called my family together into her room for prayers. We had not read half a chapter before I got up and went into her room and the death gasp had already commenced. I called my wife and family and in less than half an hour she fell asleep in Jesus.

I made her coffin myself there being no carpenter near here. She was buried on Friday about noon. Her grave is about four or five rods from the house. The brush is not cleared away more than that. My dear Sister, I have this particular in describing her case because I thought it would be gratifying to you and also that you could consult a physician and satisfy yourself more particularly about her disease if you chose.

I would add that especially in the fore part of her sickness she was tormented with intense thirst and yet she dared not drink. As soon as she drank, she vomited, and her stomach was that tender that she could hardly bear the weight of the sheet upon it. Ann was always happy and contented here.

The last thing that I remember of hearing her say about her soul before she became delirious was that she felt the witness in her soul that God had sent her here. From the time we left New York till she became delirious, there was a steady growth in grace and in the knowledge of the Gospel. There seemed to be more and more of a sinking into Jesus.

In her death you have (hole in paper) with a great loss, but it does not seem to me that mine is less. She was your child. So, she was <u>mine</u>. You gave her to me and told me to be a father to her. Whether I was or not is not for me to say but she was a <u>child</u> to me. I always called her <u>my child</u> when I spoke to her.

By her death I am left alone. My Father saw fit to deprive my dear wife of her reason so that I could not go to her to tell my trials. I could then go to Ann and find a sympathizing heart. Now I am alone. No one to whom I can unbosom my bursting heart. When Ann was with us well enough to be about the house, she was mistress of the family, and everything was in order. Now I have to the housekeeper in addition to all my other cares. My wife and Ann were like two sisters. Their souls were knit together. I sometime feared we loved her too much. God has separated us and taken her Himself and my soul says Amen. Our Father would not have taken if he had not need of her.

I will send you her chest of clothes by the first opportunity after the dry season commences. I cut off all her black hair which I will send in the chest. I am unable to give as many particulars as I wish in this small sheet. I intend to write to Mary and to Dr. Martyn. You may find things in their letters which I cannot put in here. Ann is gone we feel your loss, but our loss is her eternal gain.

Your brother in affliction,

Wm Raymond

Letter #12:

Sent from: Mende's Mission House Little Boom River, Sherbro, West Africa

Dated: August 26, 1844

My Dear Friend Mary,

On the 8th of the present month our house was visited by an angel band who without asking our leave bore on their wings the spirit of your beloved sister Ann. They left us the lifeless clay. We shed over it our tears. We clothed it in its white robe – placed it in its narrow house and buried it within sight of our dwelling. I have just been standing by the side of her grave and there tried to call to mind what I thought she would wish me to write to you. The prayers which I have heard her pour forth out of her full soul and the tears I have seen her shed in your behalf is the only apology I offer for writing to you who are comparatively a stranger to me.

From the time we left Haverhill in all her prayers in all her conversation there was one sister uppermost. The language of her soul was of that, that sister may become forever of the meek and lovely Jesus. I heard it so continually that I myself, frank in of the same spirit and almost unconsciously, began to pour out my soul on behalf of that sister.

I must not tell that that sister was Mary. You had our sister at least that loved you. And when her father called her to another part of the world, she still continued to weep for you and pray for you. Those tears are all bottled up and those prayers are all recorded and if you need them not, they must appear as witnesses against you in the day of judgment.

I have been so much in the habit of pouring my soul with Ann's in your behalf that were you my own sister I could not feel more interested in the salvation of your soul than I now do. On one occasion, when she had been praying for you, she asked if I thought she could get the witness that you would be converted. I told her yes. She thought she had exercised faith on your behalf.

Now I beseech you by all the prayers and tears of a praying mother and all the recorded prayers and bottled tears of a beloved sister who is now a glorified spirit midst the angelic host: Singing "Worthy is the Lamb that was Slain" and who now, if she could weep would again weep for you, to service at once the salvation of your mortal soul. Let all the devils in Hell- all the world – all my sins, though they be like mountains piled on mountains, appear against me in the day of judgment, but never let the prayers and tears of a praying mother and sister appear against me, never let those golden vials which are under the throne be brought to witness against me. Oh! May you by this afflictive providence be led to the feet of Jesus and like Mary of old, choose that good part which never shall be taken from you.

I have written your mother and told her all about Ann's sickness from beginning to end. I have also written Dr. Martyn and think I shall write Mr. Finney. I do not repeat in one letter what I write in another for I expect you will see them all. I found your mother's sheet too small to write all I wished. You will excuse me if I occupy the remainder of this in writing to her.

I remain yours in affliction,

Wm Raymond

My Dear Sister Harnden,

As I was unable to write all I wished in your letter I will fill out the remainder of this sheet to you. Your letter and that of Dr. Martyn came to hand the day after Ann was buried. She never heard from you form the time she left New York till she looked down from her throne of Glory and beheld your state. She often expressed a wonder that you did not write. I told her to wait, and she would see that you were not to blame. I proved so. Your letter was a day or two too late for the vessel. It was just so with a letter from my father. I never heard from home from the time I left home which was October 13th, 1843, till August 10th, 1844, and then the letter I received was written in February. Your letter to Ann I took the liberty to open to read. You will pardon me for this. I rejoice at the spirit you manifest in giving your much-loved daughter to go among the heathen. May the same God who thus sustained her, sustain you now under this still greater trial.

I regret that I write you about that expression which you made at the parting scene. I have always felt that doubtless it was the momentary bursting forth of a mother's feelings. That parting scene never shall I forget. Her death brings it up to me with all freshness of the present time. I pray to God that that scene may not be acted over at the day of judgment. I have written a short letter to Mary. I felt constrained to do. Ann's prayers and tears on her behalf constrained me. May the Lord bell this heavy stroke to the salvation of her immortal soul.

Now, my dear sister, what can I say by way of consolation? For I am myself in the same affliction. I do not mean by this that I feel the intensity of a mother's feelings. Oh no! No such thing, but I do feel that I am deeply afflicted.

I will tell you how I am. When my mind gets to pondering upon my loss, I pay a visit to Ann. I do not mean that I go to her grave, for she is not there but by faith. I visit her amidst the Father's throne. Though I am not allowed to speak to her, I can both see her and hear her. I can see that robe made so white as no fuller on earth can white be and that crown which far outshines the mid-day sun in all its splendor; be studded now and with a star and place for more to be placed there in answer to prayers yet unanswered. I can hear those soft, melodious strains that fall from her head and also that sweet voice as she tunes it to praise her dying Lord. I stand and gaze upon her. Behold all her glory. I hear the heavenly music she can now make, and my soul says it is enough. Let her stay. Praise the Lord that He has raised her from a world of sin and death to such a glorious state. 'Tis then I can rejoice in the will of my Father though it did make my heart bleed. Yes, my sister, I feel that we ought to rejoice rather that she so soon gets her crown – that she has received her reward of which you were so willing to rob her.

Our hearts must need to bleed because a wound is made and made deep. But let us go to Gilead to the Physician that is there – let us apply that heavenly balm till all is healed. Whenever you find your mind pondering upon your irreparable loss or in the least cast down, go with me by faith to those heavenly heights and take a view of the glory of your much-loved daughter. And although your heart did bleed you would give glory to God that He had taken her to Himself. Our Father does all things well. He does not willingly afflict us. When he does it is for our good.

As a mother, you will doubtless ask: did Ann have good care taken of her while she was sick? She had the best care taken of her, though some of the time, I had to divide my time between her and my wife. Then I was not always able to take good care of her as I would wish. It was then I sometimes wished you were there to take care of her. Not because I did not want to take care of her, for that was a pleasure, but because I could not take so good care of her as I wanted to. I do not think that at any time she suffered at all for the want of care. I had the three girls to assist me. Though they were very poor hands to do anything for the sick. When my wife was sicker than Ann, I slept in the room with her, and one of the girls slept in Ann's room. When Ann was sicker than my wife, I slept in the room with her. Ann used to express a great deal of gratitude to me for the good care, as she called it. I used to take care of her, and she wondered how I did so well. On one occasion, she asked me if I thought it was wrong for her to love as a father. I told her no, that as far as I filled the place of a father, she ought to love me as a father. If it was wrong for me to love her as a child I sinned greatly. My wife did not love her less than myself. We all loved. Our love was reciprocal. I found it very difficult to keep Ann from doing too much when she was unable to sit up; she would, if allowed, take her sewing to bed. Even then, she made Maria (who was particularly her girl) bring all the draws of the bureau and all the trunks and chests where she could see her and had me pack them all over, placing everything in its proper place. The little boxes, such as contained needles etc., she picked over and nicely arranged everything with her own hands.

Ann was lovely in her life and lovely in her death. A more pleasant corpse is seldom seen; I seemed as though the spirit, as it departed, left upon her countenance its own impress. As I looked at it, I could hardly make myself believe that life was not there. Ann wrote in her journal at intervals up to March 3rd. You will doubtless take a great deal of pleasure reading over what she has written. I will send it in her chest. My dear sister, you say in your letter in reference to giving up Ann to the work of a missionary that you can weep and weep and yet not murmur. May God, your heavenly father, in like manner, keep you under this still more severe trial. You will have now to call into requisition the grace of the glorious Gospel. You will now have an opportunity to test its fullness. You have been told that there was a supply for all your wants, a balm for every wound. Surely, if you find a balm for your wounded spirit, it must be a full Gospel. But you surely will find it there.

I have been called to part with Ann and, accordingly, to present appearances unless there is an alternative for the better very soon. I expect to be called to part with my dear wife. She now has severe diarrhea, which baffles all the means within my reach. Every day, she grows poorer and weaker and has less and less appetite. There is no disease so unmanageable in this country than diarrhea. The African fever is nothing compared to it. Although the Lord takes everything away, I feel I can say what the Lord gave the Lord hath taken away, blessed be the name of the Lord.

Yours in the bond of affliction.

Wm Raymond

Letter #13:

Sent from: Mende Mission House Little Boom River, Sherbro, West Africa

Dated: September 25, 1844

My Dear Sister Harnden

In my last letter to you, which bore the date of August 26th, I told you that I gave all the particulars of Ann's sickness and death. That letter was written in haste, as were all the others, and I find I omitted many things and some that were very important.

From the time we left New York, she was troubled with constipation of the bowels and, on shipboard, took physic to relieve it.

Even after that, she had that turn of the palsy (or something that resembled the palsy) she had terms of being insensible or nearly so.

When she was moved from Kaw-Mendi to the mission house, she took a cold that seemed to settle upon her lungs; she complained ever after of difficulty in her breathing.

Eliza took no cold. The reason why Ann probably caught a cold was this. As a matter of course, she was under a good deal of excitement and was somewhat delirious.

She had the impression that Eliza was very feeble and that she must take care of her, and accordingly, she exerted and exposed herself in, as she thought, taking care of Eliza when, as a matter of fact, Eliza was better able to take care of her. They were moved in the boat.

A bed was laid on the seats, and they were carried and laid into it. When they arrived at the mission wharf, they were taken out and laid in a bed in the house already prepared for them. Eliza soon, however, got up and walked around the house to see it and continued to walk about.

Ann also wanted to go around the house to see it. I told her I thought she was not able, but she thought she must see the house.

Accordingly, I assisted her to come out into the large room and front piazza. But soon, she was glad to get onto the bed again; what little strength she had was artificial. It was caused by nervous excitement.

For a day or two before she died, I would frequently have to speak to her two or three times before she would take notice – she would then start up, as it were, and ask me what I said.

Since I have written your other letter, I have thought that perhaps you would think I did wrong or at least think strange that I left Ann at all on the morning of her death when I found that she was insensible and that she breathed somewhat harder than usual.

The fact that it was by no means an uncommon thing for her to be insensible and the fact that she had been troubled with a difficulty in breathing caused one to be in no way alarmed.

As I sat upon her bedside and looked at her as I did for some minutes, I felt that her case was dangerous but not immediately so. I felt it was not impossible for God, even then, to raise her up. Little did I think the cold hand of death was already placed on her.

A few days before she died, she said to me, "My birthday comes on the 17th of this month. You will tell me when it comes, won't you?"

Before that day arrived, she was amidst the glorified throng around the Father's throne. There are no years and months with her now. It is one eternal day.

Perhaps it may sometimes cause you unpleasant feelings to think that Ann was sick and died beyond the reach of medical aid. But there are one or two things to be taken into consideration on this point.

In the first place, I have so little confidence in the physicians of Sierra Leone that if I were there, it would be with a great deal of reluctance that I should employ them at all. And then again, her disease often baffled the skill of the most immanent medical men.

I will try to send her clothes at the first good opportunity. I will send them to Brother Tappan and tell him to send them by "express" to Haverhill to Dr. Martyn. Perhaps when you receive her chest, etc., you will be surprised that I have kept nothing that belonged to Ann as a token of remembrance.

The reasons are these. She has many friends at home, and everything will be needed there, but the great and principal reason is I <u>want none.</u> I know I am singular on this point, but I never take anything as a token of remembrance. Had I taken anything belonging to Ann for a token every time my eye caught it, it would be like a knife to open my wounded heart.

I have not picked over and packed away her clothes, I will assure you, without weeping, and while I am trying to pen these lines, my heart and eyes are full. The wound is not yet healed, and I fear it will not be a long time yet to come.

I said I wanted no token of remembrance. True, I have no tangible token or keepsake, but I have some that are visible and audible. If I forget her, I am sure to bring her to mind on Saturday.

Every Saturday morning, my bed is stripped of its dirty clothes, and clean ones are put in place. This used to be done on Sunday morning. Ann introduced the custom of changing clothes on Saturday, which I intend shall be followed up at least as long as I have control of the inside of the house.

Then again, I do not think a day passed, but I heard some of her favorite hymns sung. Sarah (Margru), the one that was at Haverhill, is almost continually part of her singing, and then add to that the fact that I now occupy the same room and bed that she used to occupy and the fact that her grave is continually in my sight, and I think I need no other keepsake.

If that were not enough, the remembrance of those blessed, happy days which we have spent together will make it quite sufficient. I am almost afraid to look back and wonder if there has ever been a happier family since the primeval pair we were.

Ann and Eliza were continually singing, which made my home more than a paradise to me, and then our seasons or family devotions were nothing less than so many interviews with the God of Glory.

Ann made great progress, I will assure you- in divine life while she was with us. As a mother, you will be led to inquire what kind of coffin did Ann have. This, I know, will be a secondary thought, but it will doubtless come by. I will tell you the best way I can.

When my carpenters worked on my house, as a matter of course, I did not make any calculations for making any such thing, and consequently, I did not save the best of the boards for that purpose. In the first place, however, I would say that there was no carpenter within a long distance of us. There was but one alternative. I must make the coffin myself.

I took the best of the boards I had left, and by hard work and piecing the top and bottom, I made a coffin that, in its outward appearance, would have been respectable even in Massachusetts. I commenced it about eleven or twelve o'clock on Thursday and did not get it finished on Friday morning till after the time set for the funeral.

When I had laid the corpse into it, I changed my clothes and commenced the funeral services. I stained it black. I had no rose pink or any other color suitable. The lining on the inside was not as nice as I would have liked, but it was the best I had.

And none present except ourselves knew but what it was the best. You may ask, "What did you do for a shroud?" As you well know, I had neither the time nor the ability to make one. Eliza had some fine long nightgowns which Mrs. Tappan gave her and which belonged to her daughter, who died. I took one of those, and I thought it was respectable in appearance.

At any rate, it was the best I had or would get. For a cap, I took a very nice nightcap that had a large border and that I thought looked good. For funeral services, I read the first chapter of Job and talked for some time, sang, and prayed. We then went to the grave, and I again prayed there. The King and several of his family were present.

I sometimes wonder at myself when I look back upon my feelings at that time that I handled the corpse and made the coffin with seemingly as little feeling as though I was handling the corpse and making the coffin of a stranger.

It was not till afterward that I found how deep the wound was made. It was God that did this. If I had realized my loss at the time, it would have been impossible for me to have done what it was necessary for me to do. As it was, it took me two or three weeks to get over the effects of the excitement and hard work of that time.

Perhaps sometimes, as a mother, you may feel regret that your beloved daughter is buried so far from home among the heathen. I know well that there is a melancholy pleasure in visiting the graves of our children and of those we love and weeping over them. I have been a parent. But my sister, on the resurrection morn, it will matter but little form what part of the world our bodies rise from. You say in your letter to Ann that you feel you have but a short time to stay here. If so, you will soon meet your beloved child in Glory, where she will be able to tell you everything – far more than I can write.

It may be that the letters I have already sent may not reach you till after you receive them. I hear they were sent by way of Trinidad and fear lest they should be delayed. If they are I will say here that under date of August 26th I wrote you – Mary – Dr. Finney and Dr. Martyn with those letters are respecting Ann's death.

Since writing the above, I have felt more and more afraid, lest the letters under the date of August 3\26th would not be received at all or at least not until after acceptance of this. I would write all the particulars over again, but I have no time. I sent this to town today by a canoe.

I expect the mission boat will go to town next week, and I will try to write to you again after that. Ann died on the 8th of August 1844. Her disease was inflammation of the stomach, which was caused probably by another disease peculiar to herself (obstruction or menses). The disease was between three and four months of destructive work. Its progress was so slow and insidious that I did not consider her dangerous till a few days before her death. She had an attack of inflammation in the bowels, but by using prompt measures, it survived.

She had an attack on something that resembled palsy. At times, she lost all use of her limbs and sometimes of her tongue, and sometimes she seemed completely insensible. She has left us for a better world, but she has left a vacuum in the mission family that will not be easily filled. I cannot say anything by way of consolation, for my own heart is still bleeding.

Your Brother in Affliction,

Wm Raymond

Letter #14

Sent from: Mendi Mission House Little Boom River, Sherbro, West Africa

Dated: October 2, 1844

My Dear Sister Harnden,

I wrote you on the date of August 26th and gave you the particulars respecting the sickness and death of your beloved daughter Ann. I wrote to you again under the date September 25th and gave you further details. On August 26th, I also wrote to Mary, Dr. Martyn, and Dr. Finney, all respecting the same thing.

Those letters, I have ascertained, were all sent by way of Trinidad, and so great are my fears that they will be greatly delayed or stopped altogether that I feel it my duty to write you again and again to give you all the particulars. I very much regret that I am under the necessity of doing this, not on account of the time and paper it will take but because I know that my heart will again be laid open to its very center.

I know enough of a parent's feelings to know that if you should simply hear the fact of her death and nothing more, there would be a death-like anxiety to know the particulars. I write this letter for fear this will be the case.

Let me say that in the beginning, I wrote you as her "father" and as her physician. You will, therefore, excuse me for speaking of many things which, under other circumstances, would be a breach of propriety.

Ann died on the 8th of August last of "inflammation of the stomach." Her symptoms were obstinate vomiting, obstinate costiveness, great tenderness at the pit of the stomach, so much so that she could scarcely bear the weight of the sheet upon it, intense thirst, and yet she dare not drink for it would immediately cause vomiting, and even when she took nothing into her stomach she was tormented with empty retching.

Perhaps you may think that this disease was produced by the climate. Perhaps it was, but I never heard of it before in this country. I think there is no doubt, but it was caused by another disease that is peculiar to her sex, and I am inclined to think its foundation was laid before she reached the coast of Africa. I will give you all the particulars, and then you can judge for yourself. When she was in New York, when it was with her after the manner of women, she took a very severe cold. She said at the time and always said afterward that she did not think it materially injured her. During the passage, she was troubled with costiveness and took physics to relieve it. After leaving New York, she was not "unwell" again, but she had a fever in York. This was produced more by the obstruction than by the climate. As soon as she came "right," the fever left her, and she immediately got well and enjoyed good health till we moved to Kaw Mendi, when she had a fever again under the same circumstances. After she got up from the fever, she enjoyed tolerable health for some time, but as a matter of course, this could not long continue under such circumstances.

In the fore part of May, she had a turn of awful distress in her stomach which lasted, I should judge, nearly an hour. I gave her things that were good for colic but to no effect. At last, at her request, I gave her some cayenne pepper tea, which relieved her immediately. Even after this, her stomach never seemed to be right. She often complained of that same kind of distress, though much less severe.

On Monday, May 20th, she was taken with inflammation of the bowels. I knew this to be a dangerous disease that must have prompt and decided treatment. Accordingly, I applied a blister over the surface of the stomach and bowels. This remained on for nearly 24 hours but to no effect. The plaster had lost its strength it had been so long in this country. I then applied a mustard poultice of the same size as the blister plaster. This had all the desired effect, and she immediately got better, though as a matter of course, it left her very weak. On Sunday the 26th, she was so weak that during all the forepart of the night, I was obliged to lift her up whenever she wished to take a drink of water. At about midnight, my wife had the symptoms of approaching labor. I had feared this before on account of a severe fever which she had had under the excitement of the moment. Though so very weak,

Ann got up and dressed herself, and when the child was born, which took place about 4 o'clock on Monday morning, she took it, washed it, and dressed it. Before she got through, she sunk down exhausted upon the bed.

On Tuesday, my wife was so smart that she thought very hard of us because we would not let her dress the baby. Ann took the baby and dressed it. On Tuesday night, Ann had an attack of something that resembled palsy. She lost almost entirely the use of her limbs. On Wednesday, my wife was taken with a most violent diarrhea. She lost all power over her discharges and lay like a perfectly helpless infant in bed. Thus, I had on my hands at one time two perfectly helpless women and a seven-month-old child to wash, dress, and feed with a spoon. This was the heaviest burden my Father ever laid upon me at one time. On Friday, my wife was so bad that she thought herself, and so did I, that she would never be any better. She called the girls, and we carried Ann, who was a little better in a rocking chair, into her room, and she bid them all "farewell." At about 4 o'clock on the same day, all at once, the fever left her, and the diarrhea stopped, and she gained so fast that on Sunday, she insisted on letting her nurse the child. At last, I let her have it. She nursed it one week when she was completely exhausted and has never been well or in her right mind since.

Ann had got so much better this time that she took the child and took care of it. I told her I would take care of it, but she said I had so much to do she insisted upon taking care of it. She kept it for one week when she sunk down completely exhausted. I again took the child and the two women upon my hands and continued to have them till the Lord took the little one to himself, which took place about the first of July. During all this time, Ann was troubled with a most obstinate costiveness and vomiting and turns of the palsy or something that resembled it. Just as soon as her bowels became very much constipated, she would be troubled with the disease, which affected her in the following manner.

Whenever she made an attempt to use her hand, for instance, it would shake and twitch in all directions for a minute or so, and then she seemed to lose all power over it. When she made an attempt to drink water, her head would move with these sudden motions till it would hang down as though she had no strength to lift it. Whenever she wanted a drink of water, it was with my main strength that I gave it to her. I would sit her up in bed (she could not sit up alone), sit by her side, and put one arm around her while I gave her the water with the other. She was not able to wash herself or comb her hair for a long time. This I did for her. Sometimes, she would lose all power over her tongue and could not speak at all. Sometimes, she would be so stupid that she did not seem to take any notice of anything. When her costiveness was relieved by a physician, this complaint would also almost entirely leave her, but no sooner were the effects of the physical gone than costiveness, and this would return together. I found it very difficult to relieve her costiveness from the fact she vomited almost everything she took into her stomach. I tried everything within my power but a laxative injection, so there was no one to administer it but myself. I did not try that, for I felt that propriety would not allow it. This disease, whatever it was, left her gradually but left her mind somewhat impaired. Sometimes, she would have turned being so stupid as hardly to take notice even when spoken to, and sometimes, she seemed to run upon taking care of things. She made "Maria" (who was particularly her girl) wait upon her and bring the chests and trunks and the drawers of the bureau to the side of her bed and had her pack them all over and all the little boxes such as contained thread and needles, etc. She took them into bed and nicely packed them all over. She would sometimes be better and sometimes be worse. I looked forward to the time when she should move to our new house, a time when both she and my wife would get better at once.

At Kaw Mendi, we had nothing but a ground floor, but before the beds, I laid down boards, a mat, and a thick woolen cloth. We moved to our house on Tuesday, July 16th. As a matter of course, such an event to which we all had looked forward with so much anxiety was attended by some excitement. Ann partook very much of this and was somewhat delirious. She had an impression that Eliza was very feeble and that she must take care of her. She, therefore, exerted and exposed herself as she thought taking care of Eliza when, as a matter of fact, Eliza was better able to take care of her. In this way, she caught a cold, which seemed to settle on her lungs, and ever after, she complained of difficulty breathing, and I was obliged to keep the window up during the daytime.

Even after we moved to the Mission House, she was delirious, and her vomiting continued to increase. Her appetite seemed to fail almost altogether. I used to make her gruel out of ground rice and flour. This makes a very good gruel. From the time we moved to the mission house to her death, which was about three weeks, I hardly think she ate one quart of this gruel, and then she vomited up a great deal of what she did eat. And yet, when I would go to her and try to persuade her to eat as I often did, she would seem to think she had been eating a great deal.

For the last four days before she died, she put nothing into her stomach but water. When I would make gruel and carry it to her and try to persuade her to eat it, she would say that she was tired or that she had been eating. Sometimes, when I tried to persuade her to eat, she would say she thought I had been scolding her for eating so much. Two or three days before she died, she was taken with excessive purging "flowing." Until now, I have never considered her case as immediately dangerous. I now knew there would soon be change for better or worse. I hoped for the better but feared the worst. On Wednesday morning, that is the morning before she died, I went to her and asked how she did. She said, "Better'. I asked if she wanted anything to eat, and she nodded assent.

You can better imagine that I can describe the thrill which that word "better" sent through my soul and with what speed I made her some gruel. When I carried it to her, she said she was "tired" and could not eat then. During the last part of her sickness, she never complained of pain but of being "tired."

On Thursday morning, as soon as I perceived she was awake, I went to her and asked her how she was. She did not answer. I soon perceived she was insensible. This did not at all alarm me, for I had seen her so many times. At about 8 o'clock, I perceived she breathed a little harder than usual. This did not alarm me, for she had so often complained of difficulty in breathing. I sat on the side of the bed for some time and looked at her and thought to myself it was not impossible even then for God to raise her, for Eliza had been lower than she. I left the bedside and called my family for prayers. We had read part of a chapter when I got up and went into her room, and I found the death gasp had already commenced. I called my family to the bedside, and she died in about half an hour with her hand in mine as I sat upon the bedside. The particulars of her funeral, etc., you will find in my last undertaking under the date of September 25th, which will probably accompany this.

My dear sister, I shall not try to say one word to you by way of consolation. I cannot. My own heart has too deep a wound. She was your child, and so she was "mine." You constituted me her adopted father, and she was indeed my child, but still, there was a difference, and I sometimes think if she had so high a place in my heart who was her adopted father but a few months, how high must have been the place she had in the heart of her that bore her. You must not think that I now shall forget you. Write to me as soon as your bleeding heart is allowed.

I remain your brother in the deepest affliction,

Wm Raymond

Letter #15

Sent from: Mendi Mission House
Friday Evening
Dated: October 11, 1844

My Dear Sister Harnden,

This day has not passed without my thinking of you. Today, I have finished packing away Ann's things and am ready to send them home. Yesterday, I had them all out in the sun and partly packed them away. Today I have finished them. I could not help but think that it was just a year ago, and today, since that chest was packed in Haverhill to come to Africa, and now I have packed it to send back again but unaccompanied with the owner. This has happened without any intention on my part.

Yesterday was a good day, so I put things out to air and dry. It was not till today that I thought about it being exactly a year to a day since the chest was packed in Haverhill.

I said I had thought of you today. I thought I saw you this morning in Portland, making all possible haste to be at the depot in the season with your breast heaving with emotion which none but a mother can know. You are then borne as it were upon the wings of the wind to the embrace of your beloved daughter about to depart on the morrow. I will venture to say that it was the shortest day in your life, and every moment was improved! There were great searching of heart that day! A daughter giving up a most affectionate and tender mother and a mother giving up a most beloved daughter for Christ. What complete prostration and consecration of will to God. Angels with admiration beheld the scene. If there is anything lovely this side of glory, it is such a scene as happened a year ago today---

True, there were very strong maternal and filial affections manifested, and well, there might be – that only added interest to the scene. It showed more clearly the complete victory of the Gospel over nature. Yes, nature has its strongest ties!

I think I'll see you tonight at a late hour. The mother and daughter throw themselves upon their bed. Sleep is out of the question. There, for the last time, you pour out your souls to one another. There, the daughter received her last maternal advice. The wheels of time roll swiftly around. That was a short night. How unlike some of the days and nights which succeeded it!

Forgive me, my sister, forever thinking you gave away too much to a mother's feelings on this night when I look at the circumstances, how you were called at a moment warning to give up a most beloved daughter. I wonder how you stood the test so well. I did not then know how worthy she was of a mother's love. The victory, however, was complete. The principles of our glorious Gospel prevailed. There was a struggle, and well, there might be. Victory always implies a struggle, a struggle in proportion to the victory.

My dear Sister, I pray that the same grace that then supported you and brought you more of that conqueror through Him that loved you may now sustain you under your still more trying circumstances.

Your Brother,

Wm Raymond

Letter #16:

Addendum to:

Mendi Mission House, Friday Evening

Dated: October 11, 1844

My Dear Sister,

One word about Ann's clothes. I did intend to send home the chest as near as possible as she packed it herself, but I found it necessary to take out all the things and air them. I did intend to send home the chest and the box that you sent to her in New York, but I found that upon packing the chest over, it would hold all except her bed quilt by distributing shelves the way I have. The quilt has seen somewhat hard times since it has been here, and I felt almost ashamed to send it.

You will find but very few underclothes in the chest. The reasons are these: in the first place, she did not have a great many. She had a piece of fine cotton laid away in the draw, intending to make her some as soon as she got better. The cloth is now in the draw. In second place were some of those that had belonged to Eliza before. She (Eliza) wanted me to give back to her, which I did.

You will find but two pairs of shoes and those she had worn. The new ones which I purchased for her in New York I have not sent. There was a pair of thin slippers that she had worn, but she gave them to Eliza before she died, and Eliza now wears them. The shoes that she wore in her last sickness were those light-colored cloth ones that you would find in the chest.

I have not sent any of the things home on account of their real value, but I know it will be a great satisfaction to you and her brothers and sisters to have these things in your possession. I have, therefore, been careful to send everything that I thought would be gratifying for you to have as a keepsake. I think I have sent everything that she brought from home. That remains except the bed quilt, and I would send that were their room without.

Your brother

Wm Raymond

Letter #17

Sent from Mendi Mission House
Saturday Morning
Dated: October 12, 1844

My Dear Sister Harnden,

This is a morning never to be forgotten by you and me. You can never forget it, for on it, you embraced a much-loved daughter for the last time. I cannot forget it, for upon it, I took all the responsibilities of a father - where your duty and responsibilities ended my commenced.

A calmness and peace now rest both upon the countenance of the mother and the child. The struggle is over, and the victory is won.

I did not at that time know the value of that with which you were called to part, and consequently, I could not sympathize with you, but in your present affliction, I can, or at least I think I can. It is now over two months since that sad event happened, and yet I see not that the wound of my heart is at all healed. Neither can I yet fully realize that she is dead, though I have occupied her room and be for two months – handled over and over again the clothes she used to wear and every day beheld her grave, etc. It was only yesterday that I visited a neighboring chief on some important business in reference to the mission, and I was returning in a canoe and thinking it over to myself. The thought struck me well. I will tell Eliza and Ann when I get home. But alas, Eliza seems to take no interest in such things, and Ann--------- is not.

Sometimes, I fear we loved Ann too much. My wife, when herself, loved her as her own soul, and as for myself, I need only say she was "my child." I loved her as a child, and she loved me as a father., and we were very happy in that relationship.

Sometimes, I feel as Elihu said as he felt when he was about to speak to Job, "Behold my belly is as wine which hath no vent. It is ready to burst like new bottles. I will speak that I may be refreshed." (Job 32:19,20) One great reason why I feel Ann's death so heavily is this: my dear wife, who used to be my chief support – upon whom I used to lean and to whom I used to look as a spiritual leader is now my greatest trial.

My wife's derangement is the greatest trial, and Ann's death the heaviest stroke I ever received from my heavenly Father's hand. My wife's derangement is, as it were, like a continual running sore, while Ann's death is like a blow that seems heavier as a consequence of the sore.

My dear wife used to be a help indeed- to whom I could pour out my soul with the assurance of finding a sympathetic heart and with the assurance that my case would be carried to the throne of grace where she had power with God.

In all my acquaintance of Christians, I never saw one who had such power in prayer as my dear wife when herself. Now, I hardly dare to let her know about most trivial matters. If I do, instead of sympathy, I receive an answer, "You are the biggest fool I ever saw," or "You act like a devilish fool."

This, I know, comes from a deranged and disordered brain, but still, it is from my dear wife, and I cannot help but think of the contrast between the past and the present. She used to help me carry my load. Now, I have my load to carry alone, and she added to it.

When Ann was with us, I could go to her, and she relieved me of much of my load, but my Father has taken her, and now I am left alone, and much of the time, I feel like a bottle of "wine that hath no vent."

One thing that made Ann peculiarly dear to us was this. When she first came with us, we found her but a child in the Gospel. She had consecrated her all, yet she was but a child. Things we had learned years before she knew nothing about. But we found in her a teachable spirit, and she learned in months what it had taken us years to learn. If ever I felt happy in my life, it was in expounding it unto her the way of God more perfectly. Often, she would bring questions of duty, etc., to me. Never in my life did I see such progress made by any individual as was made by her the short time she was with us.

I thought God was preparing her for eminent usefulness in this field, but he was preparing her for himself, and she is now doubtless employed in another sphere, yet perhaps in the same field.

I do not think our work is done when we leave the body. True, our bodily labors end, but still, our spirits are engaged, I think, in the same great work of salvation. And this morning, while our hearts are bleeding on account of our loss, Ann perhaps is laboring with ten times the efficiency she would be if she were with us. Then, my sister, while our hearts are laid open to their very core and they are bleeding at every pore, let us rejoice in God who doeth all things well. Let us rejoice in the will of our Father, who does not willingly afflict his children but makes everything work together for their good.

Much has been good my soul has received from the affliction of Ann's death, and my dear wife's derangement is to me what Paul's thorn in the flesh was to him.

So that while I weep, I can rejoice. Yes, rejoice and be exceedingly glad. I can rejoice that God's will is done and not mine. I can rejoice that Ann is now in glory. Her suffering and her trials are beyond the reach of sin and Satan. I can rejoice that her crown is now made sure.

My dear sister, I have a great desire to see you. There are many things that I could tell you by word of mouth that I cannot write to you.

Should the Lord preserve my life and breath, I intend to visit America again in a year from next spring, and should you there be in the land of the living, you may expect to see me. My sister, do write to me soon. Yes, immediately. I want to hear from you very much. I want to know how you stand up under this heavy stroke. I want to know many things which I well know I cannot know till I see you face to face.

In my former letters, I endeavored to give you the particulars respecting Ann's sickness. But in them all, I forgot to say that her disease sometimes affected her eyes so that she could not tell a white man from a black man 10 feet from her. I would say here, for fear some of my former letters may fail to reach you, that I wrote you, Dr. Martyn, Mary, and Dr. Finney under the date (I think) of August 26th. These letters were sent by way of Trinidad. I wrote you again under the date of September 25th (I think) and again under the date of October 2nd. In this last letter, I repeated all of the particulars respecting Ann's sickness for fear the others would fail to reach you.

I hope you will get them all.

Your brother, as ever,

Wm Raymond

November 3rd, 1844

I am very glad to say that my dear wife is now so much better than what is written on the second page of this sheet, which will not apply to her, though she is still unable to sympathize with me. Bless the Lord, Oh my soul, for all His benefits.

Yours,

Wm Raymond

Letter #18

Sent from Mendi Mission House Little Boom River, Sherbro, West Africa

Dated: November 3, 1844

My Dear Sister Harnden,

I had about made up my mind not to write you anymore, for I fear that what I write only makes the wound of your heart still deeper rather than heal it. I am well aware that I am a miserable comforter. But there is one thing I cannot forbear to write. I have referred to it in some of my other letters but have not written it out in full. I refer to the most glorious lesson my soul has learned by this providence.

I feel now that I sinned in taking Ann's death so hard, or rather. It seemed so hard on account of my being in the wrong state of mind. I had, in fact, taken God's place and was going forward and planning for Him instead of letting him go forward and lead me.

Before we left America, I had the greatest confidence in Ann's piety and call from God to missionary work, but when I came to live with her and saw the lovely spirit she possessed, my soul became more and more attached to her every day. Not only so, but I thought I could see in her such an adaption to the missionary work, etc., that my expectations were raised high. So far, all was well. But I stopped not here; I stepped out of my place and began to plan and layout her work. Yea, more than this, I not only marked out in my own mind the path in which I expected her to walk but also the path in which I expected God to work.

I dwelt so much upon these plans in my mind that to me, they were all realities. It was confidence in my own plans rather than in God which led me to believe that Ann would not die. It was not till two or three days before she died that I felt that she was in any immediate danger. To me, her death was a most unexpected stroke, and it is but lately that my mind has recovered from the stroke so as to perceive the real state I was in.

By it all, my plans were frustrated, and I stood confounded before God. It at last led me to search my heart deeply, and I discovered the state of mind that I was in. This sunk my soul once more into nothingness, and ever since, it has been enjoying one of the richest feasts it has ever enjoyed. Christ is more precious than ever. The Bible never was such a precious book. Never before did such light beam from its sacred pages into my soul. I can see God on every page! We can never thank Him enough for such a glorious book. The character of God never seemed so glorious and lovely as now. I have never seemed so glorious and lovely as now I have such a continual sense of it that I am continually in a weeping frame. My soul, I feel, is on the advance. I feel that I am but a little child and have just commenced the Gospel alphabet.

I am so dull a scholar that it always has been by severe chastisement that my Father has taught me even the simplest lessons of the Gospel. I greatly regret that there is a necessity for this, but I still rejoice that He will condescend to teach me in any way.

I intend to go to Sierra Leone this week (unreadable), carry with Ann's chest, and have it sent home by the first vessel that sails for New York. I have taken a good deal of pains to try to get a few curiosities to fill in the crevices of the chest but have had very poor success. I have done this because I did not want an inch of room to go home unoccupied and because I know it would have been in accordance with Ann's wishes. I have taken a good deal of pains to get different kinds of termites with specimens of their nests, but having no spirits, I have been unable to preserve them. But in the attempt, I have discovered no less than seven or eight kinds. There is so much ignorance and superstition among the people about these things that it is impossible to get any correct information from them. I have tried to get you a few specimens of flowers, but it is doubtful whether I shall succeed in properly preserving them. There is a great variety of the convolvulus here, which are in almost continual bloom. The flowers in Africa generally have fine colors but no fragrance. I have found, however, a kind of pink which, though very large, has all the fragrance of our pink. I tried to preserve one but could not.

The birds here have the most beautiful plumage but scarcely one that is a good singer. I would say that termites are entirely different species from the ant, of which there is an almost endless variety.

My dear sister, as soon as you receive them, whether they were damaged, etc.,

As ever, your brother in affliction,

Wm Raymond

Letter #19

Sent Care of George Harnden

From New York, New York

Dated: December 8, 1844

Mrs. Hannah Harnden,

Georgetown, Mass.

Dear Madam,

A week or two since I heard from The Rev. Mr. Dove and the English Wesleyan missionary at Sierre Leone, and from what was said, I inferred that Mr. Raymond was alive and well. It seemed strange that no letter came from him, but the vessels that trade between this country and the Coast of Africa are so irregular that I immediately supposed Mr. Raymond had sent letters by some vessel that had a longer passage than usual. Yesterday, I received a communication from Mr. Raymond. His own health is pretty good. Though he had been sick. His wife was feeble. She had lost her little son, five weeks old. Your daughter's health has been bad for some time. Sometimes, Mrs. Raymond would be quite sick and not in her right mind. Then the care of the family would devolve upon your daughter, though she was too feeble to bear so much care. Then Mr. Raymond would get more strength, and your daughter would be quite sick and unable to do anything. Under these circumstances, Mr. Raymond had to take care of both these sick women and the little one beside them.

It is probable that I shall be able to send you more intelligence very soon, and it may be of a painful nature. The African climate is very bad for white foreigners, especially for women. Be prepared, my dear friend, for the will of God. Should we soon hear that Mrs. Raymond is no more or that your beloved Ann has been removed to another and a better world, may we all - may you - be enabled sweetly to acquiesce in the will of God, our Father, who orders all things in mercy. To Him, I commend you and yours.

Lewis Tappan

(Margin)

Your daughter has had the fever twice- then inflammation of the bowels – then constipation of the bowels, etc., etc. Her strength and Mrs. Raymond's were greatly reduced, and the worst consequences were feared on account of both these dear saints.

Letter #20

Sent from New York, New York

Dated: December 10, 1844

Mrs. Hannah Harnden

Georgetown Mass.

Dear Friend,

Enclosed is a letter from Wm Raymond. It contains heavy tidings for you. May God give you grace to bear patiently what He, in infinite wisdom, sends upon you. Our children are not our property but His. He gave, and He has a right to take away. Blessed be His name! I pray that you may have rich consolation in Christ Jesus. Your Ann has not lived in vain. Precious in the sight of the Lord is the death of his saints. I hope you will be able to rejoice that you had a daughter to yield up to the Lord – to go as a missionary – and to live a holy life and die a happy death on a missionary ground. Such is not the privilege of all parents. May the Lord abundantly bless you and yours.

Your sympathizing friend,

Lewis Tappan

Letter #21

Sent from New York, New York

Dated: December 14, 1844

Mrs. Hannah Harnden

Georgetown, Essex Co. Ms.

Dear Madam,

The Executive Committee of the Union Missionary Society, at their monthly meeting last evening, directed me to write to you a letter of sympathy and condolence on account of the removal of your dear daughter from her missionary field on earth to the rewards and employment of heaven. The committee is deeply affected by a sense of the loss the mission has sustained by the early death of your daughter Ann, but they consider that it is the act of Him who never errs, who does not willingly afflict nor grieve the children of men, and who brings lasting good out of seeming evil. We rejoice that God gave you such a daughter, that she was willing to embark for a foreign country in the missionary service, and that she exhibited so bright an example, even for so short a period, in the vernal darkness of a heathen land. We deeply sympathize with you, dear sister, in your affliction and pray that God may sanctify this event for you and your family. We commend you to Almighty God and pray that when He shall dismiss you from the trials of life, you may be permitted to join your sainted daughter in the realms of bliss. We ask your prayers for us, for the Mission, and for the poor heathen.

With much respect,

I remain on behalf of the Committee respectfully and affectedly yours,

Lewis Tappan,

Cor. Sec.

Mr. Raymond allowed me to read the letters he addressed to you and his other friends in this country and to make such extracts for publication as appeared but, which you and the other friends will, I trust, approve. I will soon send you a **Union Missionary - Extra,** *containing extracts from Mr. Raymond's letters.*

Letter #22

Sent from Mendi Mission House

Dated: January 13, 1845

Dear Sister Harnden,

Today, I have been looking over my old papers, and I accidentally met with this, which I sent you. It was written in the following manner. When we were on shipboard, I told Ann that she must write you a long letter. I told her if she would write, I would write it over and correct the grammar, etc., and then she must copy mine and send it to you. She wrote from day to day when we arrived at the Gambia, and I wrote it over on this sheet, correcting the grammar and placing capitals right.

When she wrote you at the Gambia, she had little time, and another thing, she was on shore, and this sheet was on board. I tried afterward to make her copy it, add to it, and send it to you, but she never did entirely.

I put it among the duplicates of the letters I wrote on board, and today, as I was looking for them over, I found it. It was some time before I could call to mind its whole history. What alterations I made in it I cannot now tell, but it is doubtless indebted to me for some of its grammar, but the composition was entirely hers. The reading of it has brought my mind many painful and pleasing recollections.

My wounded heart, I sometimes think, has got well and healed, but to this day, I cannot bear to see Ann's name on anything that belonged to her. Her grave is ever in my sight, and let one day here that not a weed or blade of grass is allowed to grow upon it and a path is always kept clean from the house to it. This had been done by Daddy George without my direction.

When I was ordered by the king to leave this place, there seemed nothing so dear to me as those two graves (Ann's and little Charles Finney's), I mean of a worldly nature, and had I been able to take nothing else, it seemed as though I must take them.

May the Lord be with, strengthen, and bless you under all of your manifold trials ----- is the prayer of --

Your brother in Christ,

Wm Raymond

This letter was in the trunk with Ann's lost letter.

Letter #23

Sent from Mendi Mission House, Little Boom River, Sherbro, West Africa

Dated: August 8th, 1845

My Dear Sister Harnden,

Although we are this day separated thousands of miles apart, in different climes, in different parts of the globe with boundless deep rolling between us yet, such has been the sameness of our minds that without doubt, we have been pondering over the self-same thing.

A year ago, today in this house, I closed in death the eyes of one who for many years had called you "Mother" and who for a short time had looked to me as a "father."

Eternity alone will be able to reveal the depth of the wound my heart then received, and it was impossible that this anniversary should pass without my noticing it.

Although some months elapsed before the news of this day's work crossed the trackless main and plunged the fated dagger into your heart, yet I will know this anniversary had not passed without your mind unconsciously pondering upon the sad event.

I cannot write. I take up my pen and lay it down. I take it up and lay it down without making any progress at all. It is so impossible to pour out a wounded heart on paper. What plunged the dagger so deep in my heart was my exceeding high anticipations of her future usefulness, and these continued till but a day or two before her death. I never think of her without a reproof coming as it were from the very throne of God, which seems to say, "Never plan for God again."

Though one year has passed, and that little room in which that spirit took its flight is very much altered and enlarged (so that instead of its being 10 ft by 12 ft, it is now 14 ft square) yet, from time to time, I unconsciously trace out with my eyes in the floor- the very spot on which the bed used to stand.

August 9th. It is a year ago this day since we committed to the dust the remains of the one we loved. In memory of that sad event, I have this day had stones placed at the head and foot of the grave. This, you may think, should have been done long ago, but stones are very scarce here. The one at the head is a hewn one and was brought from Sierra Leone in my canoe. Where the other came from, I cannot tell.

Unless you or some of your friends prefer to do it yourselves, I intend to get some gravestones at the Mission's expense whenever I go home. I have not yet decided upon the spot for a burying ground. After this is done, I shall have the remains dis-interred and interred in the burying ground.

I feel very anxious to hear from you. I want to know whether you received her chest safely or not and whether you found everything inside correct. I took a great deal of pains to have them so. There were several articles left by mistake, which I will bring when I come. I find among my letters one which I received from Ann. I will send it to you when I have the opportunity.

Letter # 24

Sent from Freetown, Sierra Leone

Dated: September 28th, 1845

My Dear Sister,

We were made exceedingly glad on the 6th instant by the reception of your kind letter dated April 22nd, 1845, and also one from Dr. Martyn dated April 24th. I have not received a letter for a long time, which did me so much good as that. I felt the need to praise God for His grace in sustaining you in such a wonderful manner under your severe affliction. I felt that your heart and mine sympathized together. It must have been a solemn occasion when Dr. Finney preached the funeral sermon.

I am exceedingly glad that you received her chest safe and think that the things were not injured. I felt very sorry that the hair did not look natural- I took a great deal of pain with it. Just before the chest was put on board the vessel, I took it out and looked at it. I have been sorry since that I did not unbraid it and comb it. I thought of it, but my feelings were against it. I always combed it for her when she was sick, and I felt the associations were such that I could not. I am sorry now that I did not. You seem to anticipate a great deal of pleasure in seeing me. I will assure you that you do not anticipate more than I do in seeing you. I have expected all along that I should spend the summer of 1847 in America, but there seems no probability of their sending many colleagues at present, and I know not when I shall be allowed to leave the Mission. The mission had passed through very severe trials, but its prospects were never so promising as at present. The Lord is with us.

My own health is excellent, for which I feel the need to praise the Lord. My dear wife's health has been better during the last rains than it ever has been before the rains. Her mind, however, has not been right at all times, and then sometimes I have my fears. This is my greatest trial, but it has been for my good; I have learned a great deal of patience. It is true that God permits nothing to happen to his children but what is for their good and His glory. The Bible was never as precious to me as it is now. It is indeed the Book of Books.

We came up to Sierra Leone about two weeks ago. When I am here, I do not generally have much time to rest. A week ago, last Sunday, I was at York, and I preached twice. On Monday, I married nine couples. On Wednesday, I came to town and went to chapel with the expectation of preaching, but it was too late. On Thursday night, I preached. It is on Sunday twice and every night this week. Today is Friday. I send you a paper. I wrote the pieces signed "Anti-slavery," "Candour," and the "Illustration of the Scripture." I was the preacher there spoken of.

This paper upon which I write is some which Ann's cousin Moses? (Morris) Greenleaf gave to her. If you compare it with that which she wrote to you, I think you will find it the same. There will be another vessel sailing in a few days. I will try to write to Dr. Martyn. In the meantime, give him and his family our love.

Mrs. Raymond and I are now at the Wesleyan Mission House, where we are quite at home. We expect to stay a week or two longer and then return to the Sherbro. "No place like home." I came up to purchase provisions and to make arrangements for my dry season work. If I ever come to America, and you are in the land of the living, you may expect me to come to see you.

I can hardly tell the reason, but it seems almost as though I belonged to your family. When I shall come, I cannot tell. I cannot come till somebody comes to help me. I cannot leave as soon as one comes but must stay one rainy season with him before I think it best to leave him. Not everyone can stand the climate as I do. The Lord is exceedingly good to me.

My dear wife wishes to tell you that she has felt very deeply for you on account of Ann's death. She says she feels Ann's loss very much. She is so lonesome in the country without a white woman within 100 miles. But she says her loss is Ann's eternal gain. I often say she thinks of her in the presence of God and thinks how glorious she appears and how I shall soon be with her to part no more.

I feel, says she, that my soul is becoming more and more fit for the Kingdom of Heaven. She sends her warmest love to you, which, let me join. Do not fail to write me again soon. I shall always be glad to hear from you. Don't forget to write me soon.

Remember us fondly to all your family.

Your brother

Wm Raymond

Letter #25

Lewis Tappan, Esq. New York

Dear Sir,

I received and accepted with thanks the elegant Bible, presented to me by Cinque, Kinna, Kale, and the thirty-two other Medians, who are indebted to you and your benevolent associates, probably for their lives, certainly for their deliverance from unjust prosecution and long protracted imprisonment and finally for the means of returning to their own country....[I] hope for the consummation of your kindness to them in the accomplishment of their restoration in freedom and safety to their native land. I am, with great respect, dear sir, faithfully yours,

JOHN QUINCY ADAMS

www.ingramcontent.com/pod-product-compliance
Lightning Source LLC
LaVergne TN
LVHW061034070526
838201LV00073B/5029